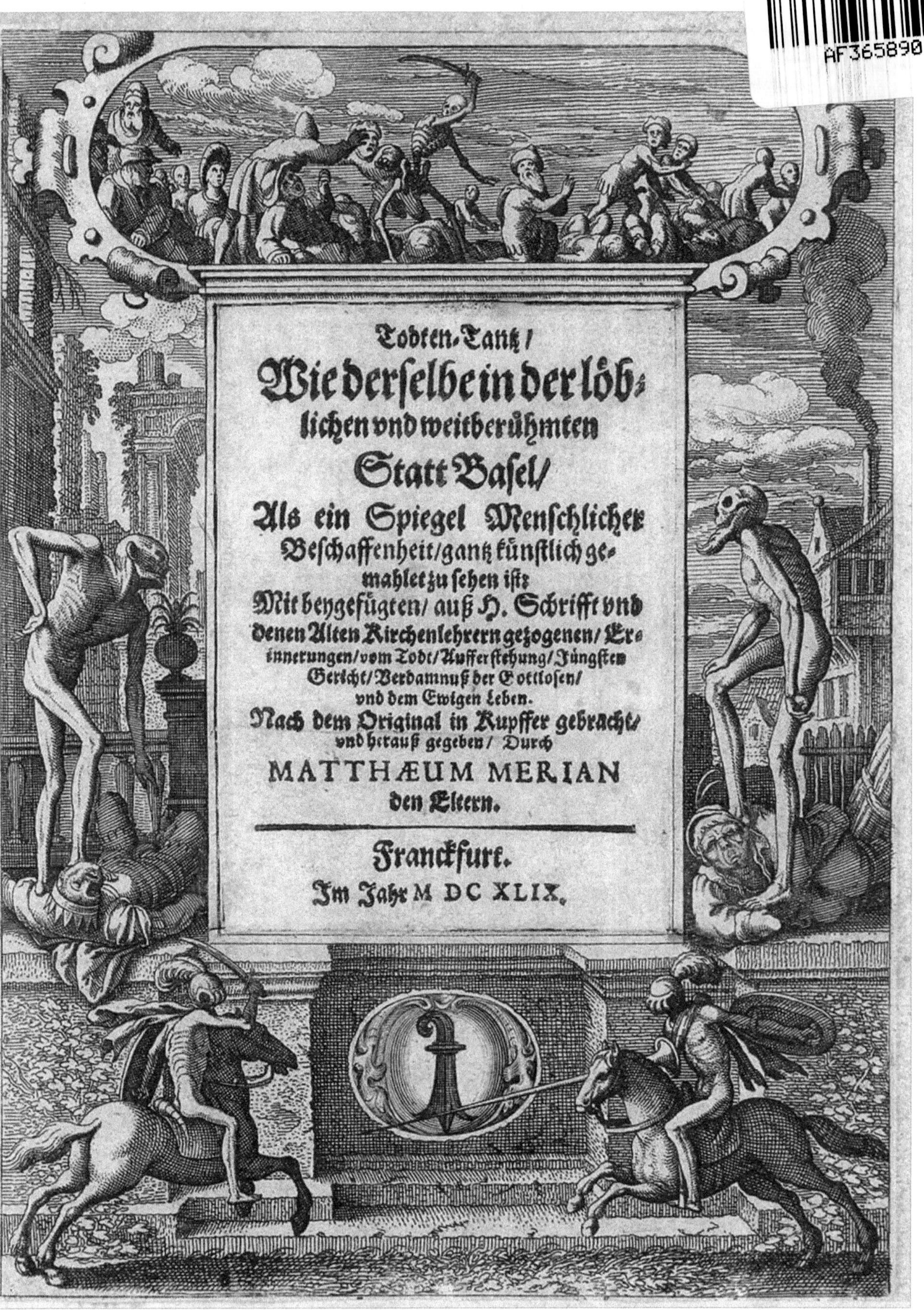

Todten-Tantz/
Wie derselbe in der löb-
lichen vnd weitberühmten
Statt Basel/
Als ein Spiegel Menschlicher
Beschaffenheit/gantz künstlich ge-
mahlet zu sehen ist:
Mit beygefügten/ auß H. Schrifft vnd
denen Alten Kirchenlehrern gezogenen/ Er-
innerungen/vom Todt/Aufferstehung/Jüngsten
Gericht/Verdamnuß der Gottlosen/
vnd dem Ewigen Leben.
Nach dem Original in Kupffer gebracht/
vnd herauß gegeben/ Durch
MATTHÆUM MERIAN
den Eltern.
Franckfurt.
Im Jahr M DC XLIX.

Title: **DANCE OF THE DEATH** - **Danza macabra - Danse des morts, Todten-Tantz von der stadt Basel**
By Matthäus Merian and Luca Stefano Cristini

ISBN code: 978-88-93272254 First edition March 2017
Code.: **MUSEUM-001**, Editorial series code: **MISTERY-001**

Cover & Art Design: Luca S. Cristini & Anna Cristini
MUSEUM brand is a trademark of Soldiershop publishing, via Padre Davide, 7 - 24050 Zanica (BG) ITALY.
www.bookmuseum.it

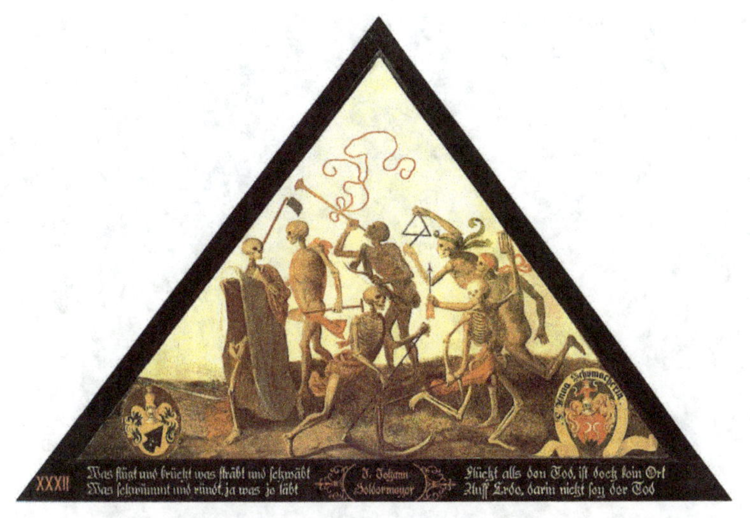

DANCE OF THE DEATH

DANZA MACABRA - DANSE DES MORTS
TODTEN-TANTZ VON DER STADT BASEL

*

BY MATTHÄUS MERIAN
THE ELDER (1593-1650)

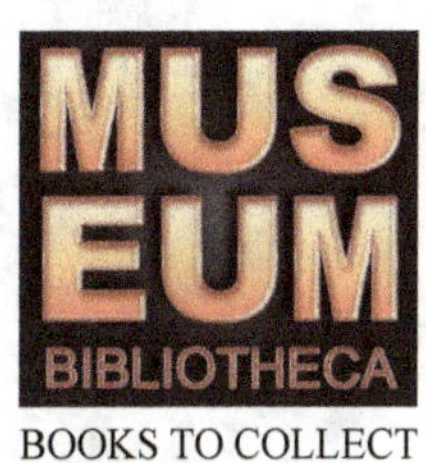

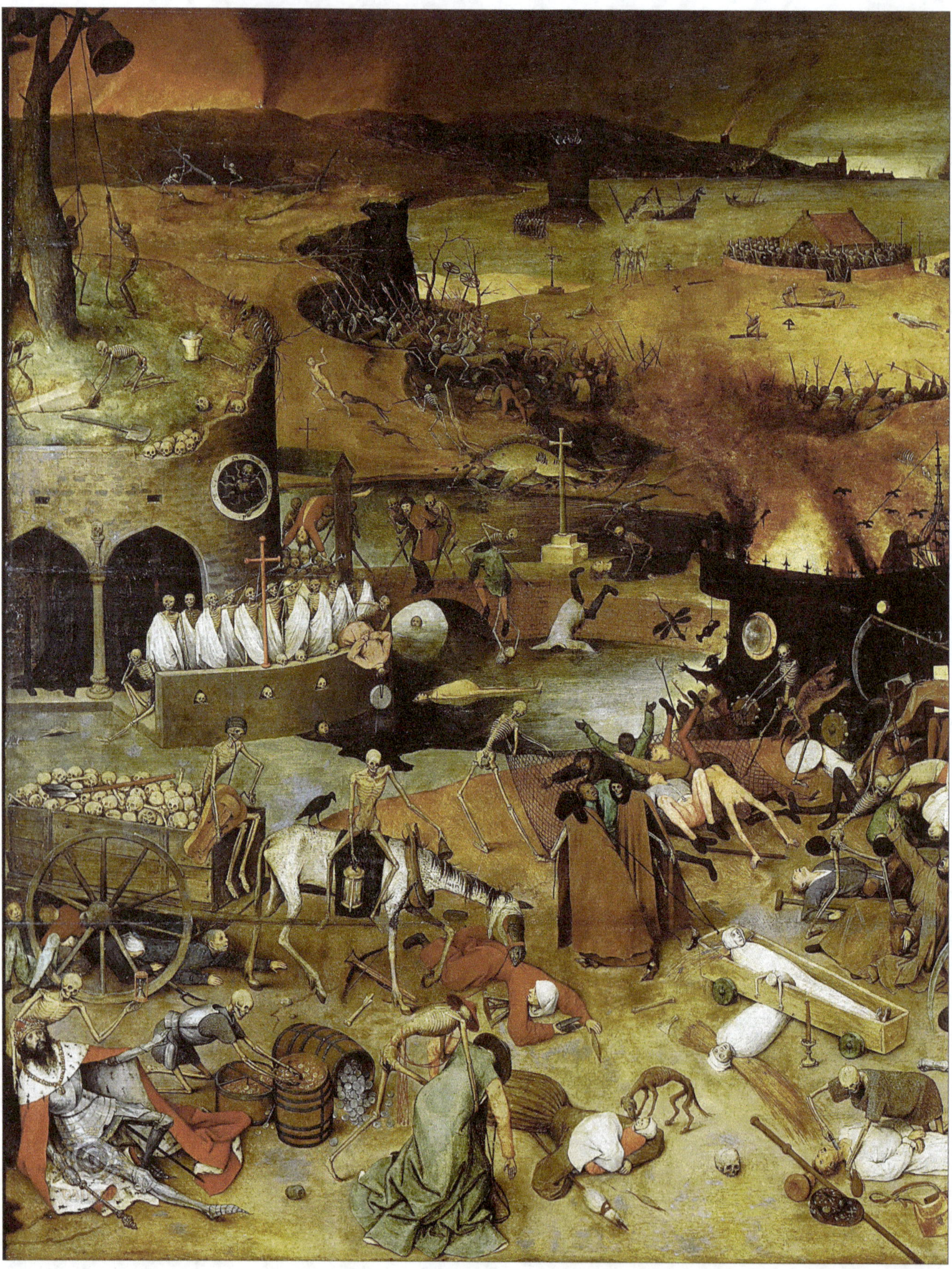

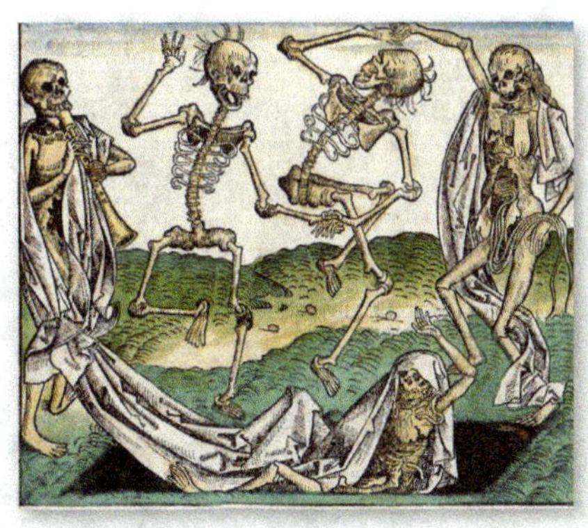

DANCE OF THE DEATH - DANZA MACABRA - DANSE DES MORTS - TODTEN-TANTZ

The Dance of Death, also called *Danse Macabre* (from the French language), is an artistic genre of late-medieval allegory on the universality of death: no matter one's station in life, the Dance of Death unites all.
The *Danse Macabre* consists of the dead or personified Death summoning representatives from all walks of life to dance along to the grave, typically with a pope, emperor, king, child, and labourer. They were produced as *mementos mori,* to remind people of the fragility of their lives and how vain were the glories of earthly life.

Our **Museum book** are a fine reproduction of a complete engraved title-page and 44 engravings in the text (complete with the 2 full-page plates *"Memento mori"* and the transformation portrait showing the death of Dives), all finely colored in a contemporary hand.

From a XVII century edition Published by Matthäus Merian the Elder. A work preserving a visual record of the famous Basel wall-paintings depicting a Dance of Death cycle. Dating from the 15th century, they had undergone restoration in the 16th and early-17th centuries.

Merian added the *"Memento mori"* plate as well as the famous final "puzzle" engraving which can be viewed from two directions.

Our book presents all the text of the plates in English, French and Italian language.

◄ *Pieter Brueghel the Elder, The Triumph of Death (c. 1562 particular) in the Museo del Prado, Madrid.*

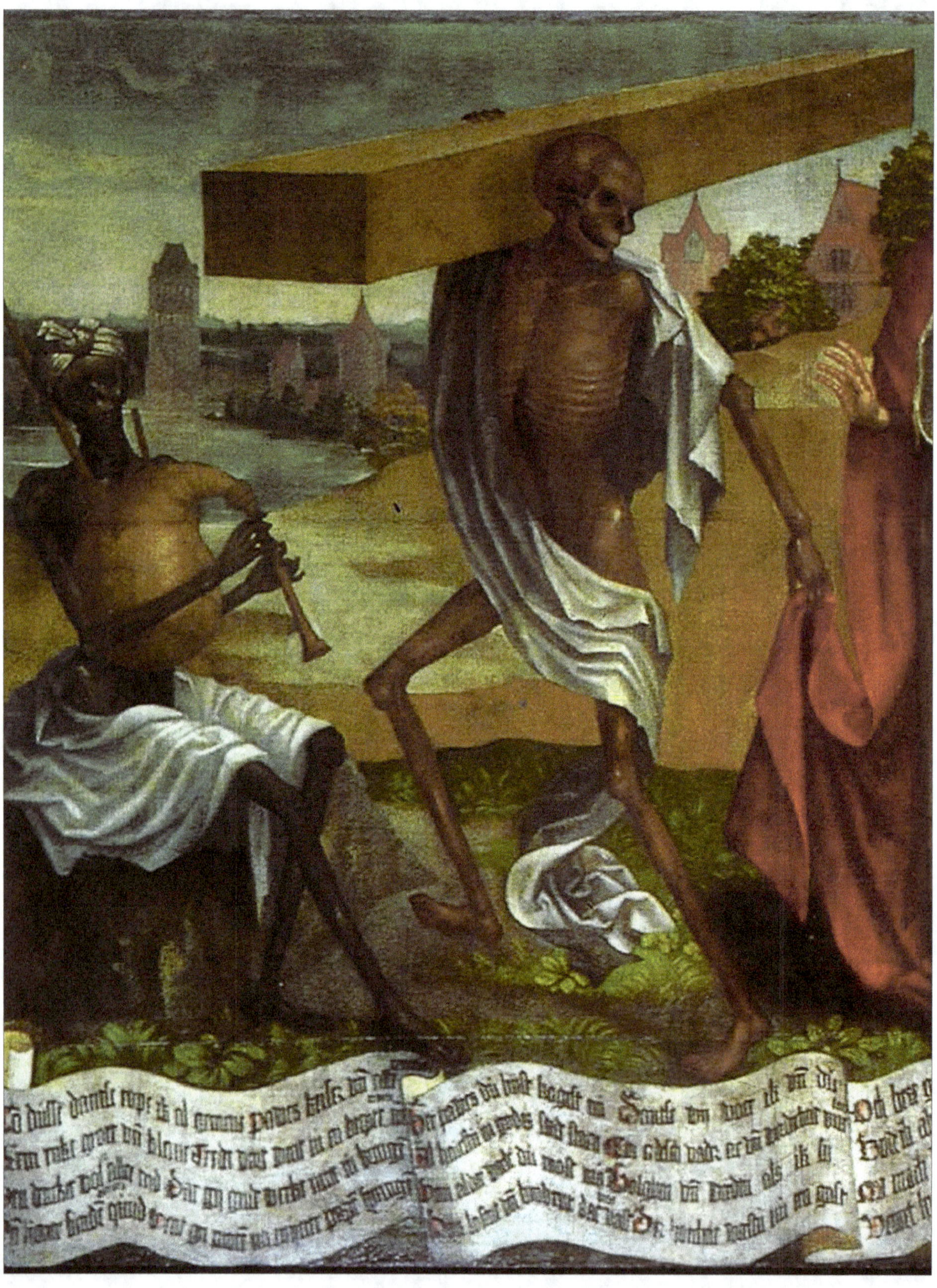

THE BASEL DANCE OF DEATH BY MATTHÄUS MERIAN THE ELDER

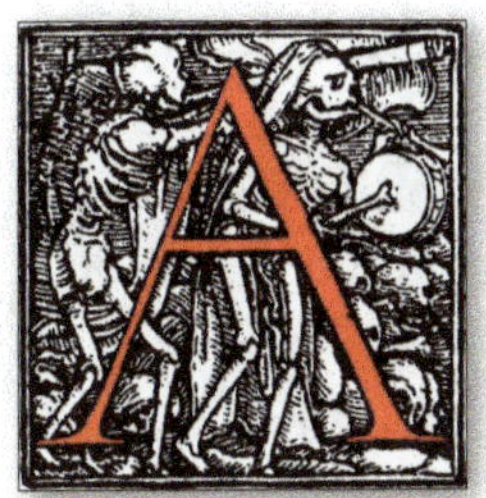

number of ideas, now poignant, now powerful and even profound, are associated with the thought of Death, and our gravest meditations are always connected with it in one way or other.

It is the invisible center around which the most important questions revolve; the gloomy problem which we endeavor to solve in the great enigma of life; the difficulty, the removal of which would introduce order, unity and clearness into our system of thought and into the development of our active existence.

The followers of a purely terrestrial philosophy harass themselves in vain to raise the impenetrable vail, behind which a bottomless abyss must lie, or an endless expanse be spread out. Some, unable to remove the vail and unwilling to trust to faith in their anxiety, endeavor to prove, that we should occupy ourselves with thinking of that, which but oppresses the soul; while others strive to reconcile the spirit to the thought of death, and in all seriousness extol! the dull witticism of some dramatist *"To die is nothing, 'tis but the last hour of existence."*

Others, lastly, with more sense, but without any better success than the first, ridicule these vain endeavors, and assert that there is no one on the face of the earth, who is not afraid of death. All without exception give evident proof, by the care with which they treat of it, that this subject is just as important for them as for the rest of their fellow-men, and all miss the mark, because they know not the voice of Him, who bath brought life and immortality to light.

But, among all the agitating and alarming thoughts, which the remembrance of death calls forth, there is one that, above all others, is comforting to men, and which is seized upon by the poor and unhappy with a certain malicious pleasure; viz, the thought, that by death the primitive equality of the human race will be restored.

This thought, cherished at all times by the people, was more especially so at a time, when mankind was divided into two great classes, the oppressors and the oppressed.

And when, in the medieval age, one of those physical scourges, which gradually gave way before advancing civilization, demanded indiscriminately its tribute of slaughter from all ranks of that enormous human mass, which was held together by the feudal system, for want of a better social organization; the common people took some pleasure in spite of their own loss in the general evil, which produced a certain equality between them and their tyrants, as it distributed ruin with impartial hand; and this secret delight in destruction, joined with the austere religious principles and gloomy disposition of the monks, gave rise to those remarkable productions, known under the name of *"Dances of Death"* the true representation of one of the

◄ Danse Macabre in in St. Nicholas' Church, Tallinn (particular) by Bernt Notke (1440-1509)

most celebrated of which we now present to the public.

This *"Dance of Death"* was long ascribed by general consent to Holbein, as it was formerly the custom to give the credit of all the fine paintings in his native town to that celebrated artist.

This error, produced another , which is an example, among others, of the strength of preconceived opinion.

It was imagined that the characteristic strokes and peculiar merit of his pencil, were to be discovered in these pictures, while is was forgotten, that in addition to their marked inferiority, the costume and other circumstances give proof of a much earlier origin.

At the present day, no more doubt is entertained upon the subject, and to Holbein is scarcely conceded the honour of having touched them up - an honour, by the way, of which Holbein's fame does not stand in need.

Holbein did indeed design and execute a *"Dance of Death"* which was beautifully carved in wood, most probably by Hans Leutzelburger, surnamed Frank.

Several editions appeared of it, all of which however are now scarce. These may be seen at the library of the Frankfurt university, as well as another, in which the figures are inserted into the initial letters of the alphabet , and which is cut out with extreme delicacy in wood by the same artist. It appears from the research of several critics, that the custom of painting on the walls of cloisters and in the vaults or places of interment, a series of pictures representing Death, bearing away human beings of all ranks, was common as early as the 14th century and perhaps

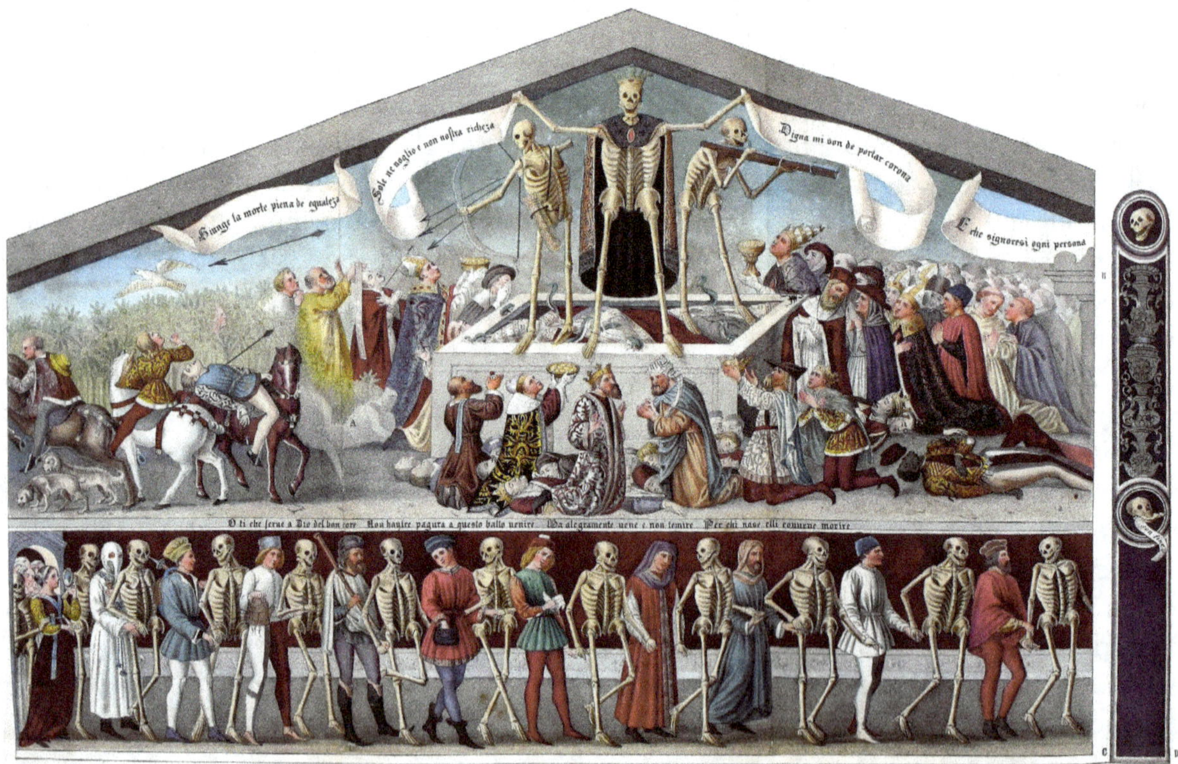

▲ *The "Danza macabra" of oratorio dei disciplini in Clusone (Bergamo) North Italy*

even earlier. Some are of opinion that this idea took its rise in the mummeries of this description, which were common at the time of the carnival; others, that the immense depopulation caused by the plague, then so frequent in Europe, was the origin of these singular paintings.

Whichever of these opinions we may adopt, so much is evident, that the unwonted spectacle of mortality, which the middle ages but too often presented, contributed directly or indirectly to produce them, and it is of little importance to know whether the commencement was made by personal representations or by pictures in the strict sense of the word.

During the time of the Council of Basle, the plague raged; in remembrance of which, the Dominican friars; and according to some the Fathers of the Council themselves, caused a *"Dance of Death"* to be painted on the inner walls of the burial ground of St. John's Church, as an instructive and edifying memorial of those days of visitation.

It was however, in all likelihood, merely a copy of the one which might be seen, at an earlier period in the nunnery of Little Basle, the present Klingenthal.

The name of the painter is unknown, and we only know that a. d. 1568 Hans Hug Klauber was commissioned to touch up the pictures, the colours of which had begun to fade.

Finding a few empty spaces, he represented at the commencement of the series, the reformer Oekolompadius, then still alive, as preaching on Death and the Last Judgment to a number of men of all ranks; and at the end of this funeral concourse the artist represented himself, as reminded by Death, that soon he must follow those, whose images he had been renewing. The last picture executed by him, is that of his wife and child, receiving from Death the same invitation.

About this time the rhymes, which may be read above and under each scene, appear to have been composed. Indeed, how can we suppose, that these verses were written at the time of the Council. It was enough to represent the grandees of the world and the rulers of the Church as the victims of Death, that sweeps them away along with the meanest mortals.

Tills cutting satire is certainly not the least important, but it does not strike directly home, the rhymes, on the other hand, contain too plain a mockery as to admit the supposition, that they were written at the time, and so to speak under the very eyes of the Council.

Doubtless the dignitaries of the Church were not spared in the literary productions of that period, as the Fabliaux testify; but it may with justice be doubted, that an assembly of Cardinals and Bishops would have permitted, and that Dominican friars would have commanded, that this satire should be rendered solemn and perpetual.

It is therefore much more natural to believe that these verses were written at the time of the Reformation. Besides these rhymes manifest but little talent, contain but a very limited number of ideas, and repeat continually the same thought, which they modify to suit the condition of each individual in turn, in our modern edition, we present them in English, French and Italian verse, giving as near as possible the substance of each stanza.

These pictures have several times been renewed (a.d. 1616 and 1658), but at the commencement of XIX century they were found injured to such an extent, that the wall, on which they were executed, was not considered worth the ground it occupied.

It was therefore removed in the year 1805, after an attempt had been made to preserve those portions which were in a better condition, some of which may still be seen in the council-salon

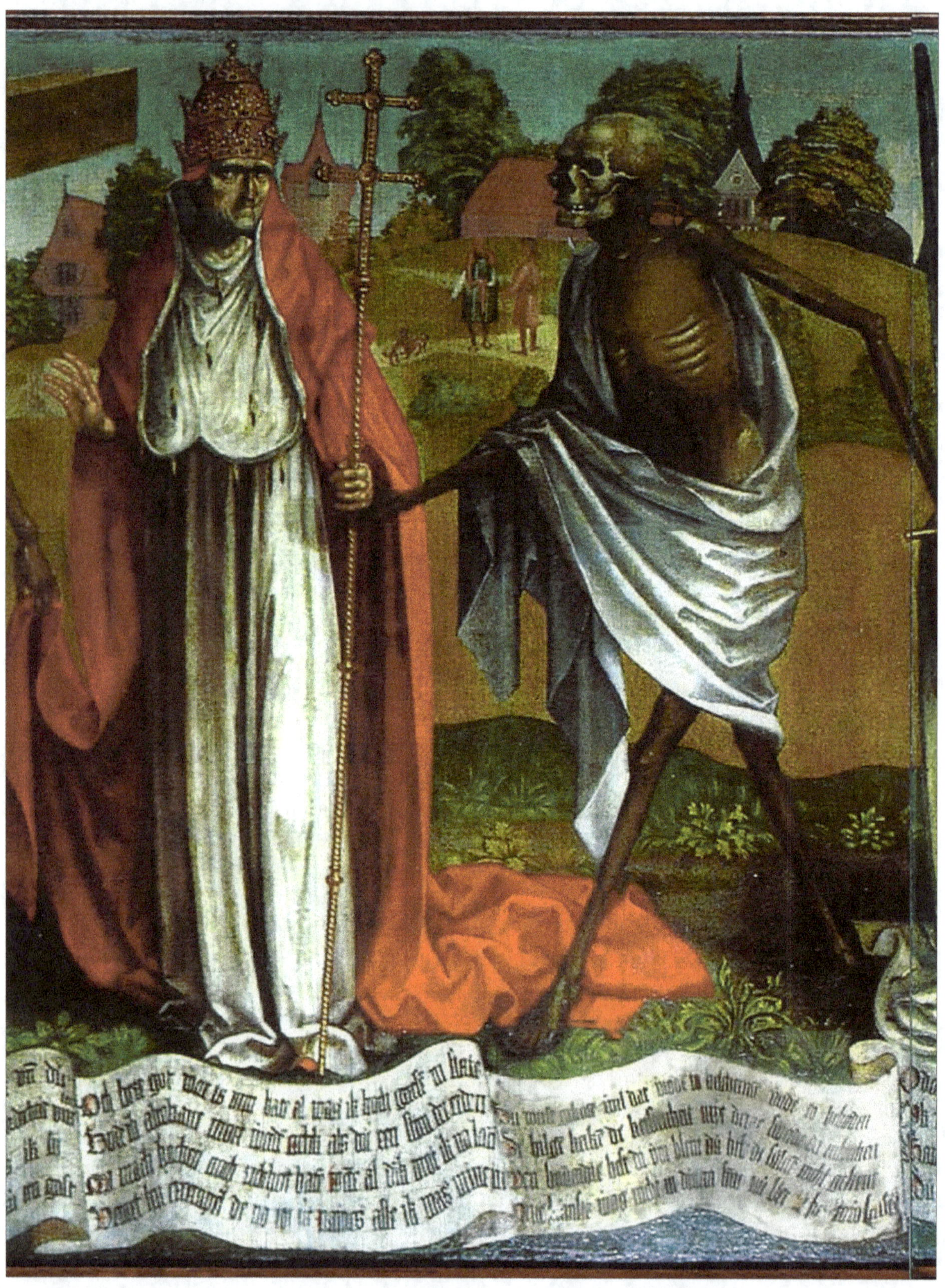

of the Basle cathedral. The piece of ground on which the *"Dance of Death"* formerly stood, was converted into a promenade, which still retains the sad appellation of its ancient celebrity. Matthew Merian, a clever engraver made and published, towards the middle of the 17th century, a series of prints, copied from the 42 paintings of the "Dance of Death", along with a voluminous collection of historical proofs, edifying reflexions and religious hymns annexed to each separate picture.

During the years 1744 and 1789 two new editions of these engravings were made, the plates of which are still used. We know also the same engravings neatly colored, after a drawing taken from one of the original pictures.

Nicholas Manuel painted a *"Dance of Death"* on the walls of the Dominican monastery at Berne about the beginning of the 16'" century, which is distinguished by a remarkable originality of thought and liveliness of coloring, and which has been lately lithographed and published.

In no age but a barbarous one, when the truths of the Gospel had been disfigured by superstition, could Death be represented in a form as hideous as in these pictures.

The ancients, who but rarely painted skeletons, because they are not fit subjects for the fine-arts, never thought of representing the abstract idea of death under such a repulsive form.

A genius extinguishing a torch, a figure sunk in profound repose: such were the lineaments, by which they represented that solemn and last event of human life.

And when they wished to represent the souls on their journey to the dark abode, they represented Mercury, the messenger of the Gods, carrying instead of his accustomed caduceus an ivory wand, about to deliver, at the command of Jupiter, the God of life, the souls to his brother, the sovereign of the dead.

We, however, follow the barbarous imagination of our ancestors, or rather, we are restricted to it; for a skeleton is our only form to represent Death; and the repugnance of this idea causes us often rather not to attempt to paint death at all.

And you it would seem, that the worshippers of a revelation, which has removed the sting of death and overthrown the victory of the grave, should be able to depict with more noble features and in a more touching manner, that earnest dispensation of the God of the living.

Which concludes at one stroke the severe and important trials of the creature, in order to transport it at once from the place of its exile to the bliss of eternity.

An Angel with grave but compassionate mien, bearing in one hand an extinguished torch, in the other a second which be has just kindled in heaven, would exhibit death with more fidelity for the Christian, than such ghastly figures, which belong to dead bodies but not to Death.

Whatever may be the private opinion of each on this subject, all must at least confess, that the execution is far from being without merit. The designer of these paintings was assuredly a man of genius, and one by no means destitute of poetical talent.

The expression, which he bas been skillful enough to introduce into those flesh-stripped countenances, is deserving of attention, The diversity of posture and motion in all these images of Death, the clever manner in which Death is made to play his part with many of his victims, as for instance, with the monk, with the duchess, with the blindman, with the cripple and

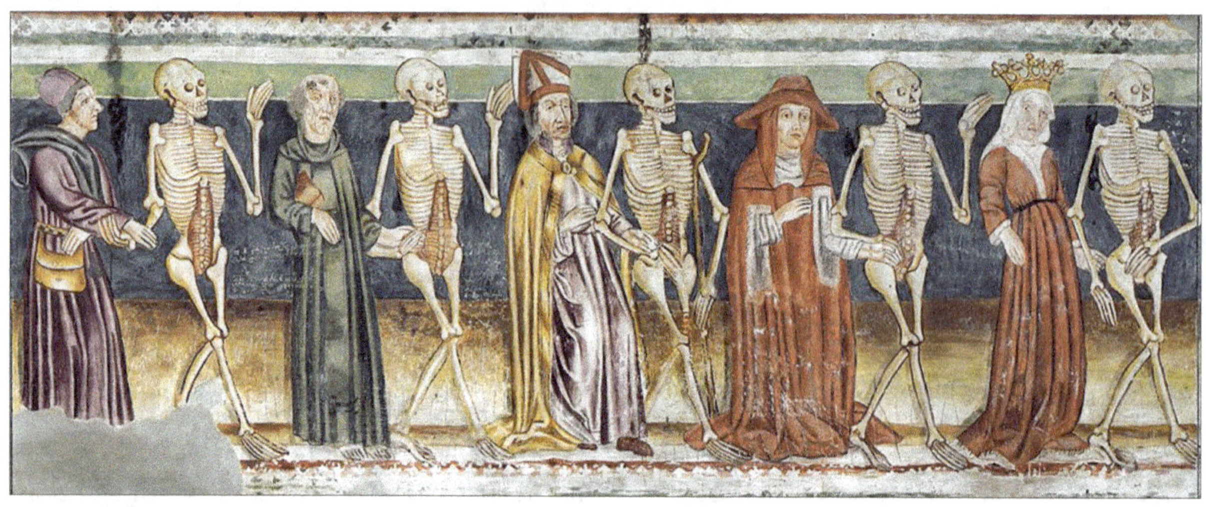

< feature/>▲▼ *Dance of Death (replica of 15th century fresco; National Gallery of Slovenia)*

with the doctor, (to whom he appears as a flesh less frame, as if to give him a last anatomical enjoyment); and lastly, the young lady, who is allowed to see her impending transformation in a mirror; all these niceties give proof of genius and talent, and even the figures of the mortals themselves, although not of equal merit with regard to comic force, have often all expression at once genuine and appropriate.

Although the "modern" XIX century critic of the fine arts, cannot look at these pictures with the same admiration, with which our ancestors regarded them, yet nevertheless, he will find them well worthy of attention, and will appreciate our undertaking, which has for its object the revival and extension of one of the most characteristic monuments of the middle ages.

(text present in the original XIX century book)

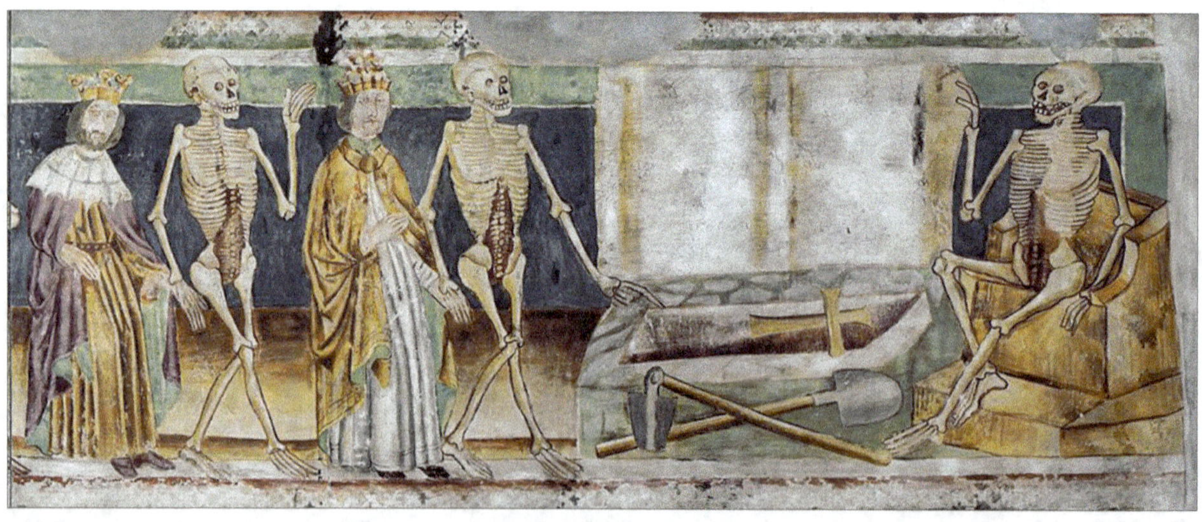

MATTHÄUS MERIAN THE ELDER

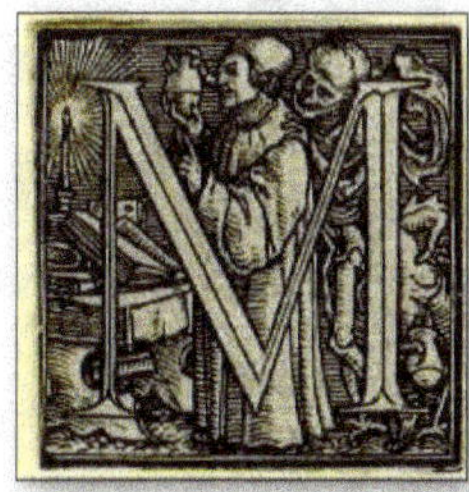

atthäus Merian der Ältere (or "Matthew", "the Elder", or "Sr."; 22 September 1593 – 19 June 1650), was a Swiss-born engraver who worked in Frankfurt for most of his career, where he also ran a publishing house. He was a member of the patrician Basel Merian family.

One of the most important draftsman and copperplate engravers and publishers of the 17th century.

He first learned the glass painting craft, but soon turned to etching.

It has been proved that he was Dietmar Meyer's apprentice in Zurich from 1610, but in 1611 he was already working for the Duke of Lotharingia.

From 1612 to 1615 Merian was working for the French court before he returned to Basel. After trips to Swabia, Augsburg and maybe Nuremberg, Merian began to work for Jan Theodor de Bry's (died 1623) publishing company in Oppenheim, and later became his son-in-law. Together with de Bry, Merian subsequently worked in Heidelberg for 2 years, before he returned to Basel with his family in 1620.

After moving to Frankfurt in 1624 Merian mainly worked in the publishing business and focused his etching on cover illustrations for the books he published, several fliers and paintings for the Habsburg royal family.

He produced, with help from assistants, numerous engravings of battles and hunts, and topographic prints of European towns.

Merian became famous for the cityscapes he produced for Martin Zeiler's *'Topographia Germaniae'* from 1640, which have a high documentary value.

His illustrations for 'Theatrum Europaeum' realized in several volumes, are also very famous.

After his death, both works were carried on by his sons Matthäus the Younger, Kaspar and Maria Sibylla Merian.

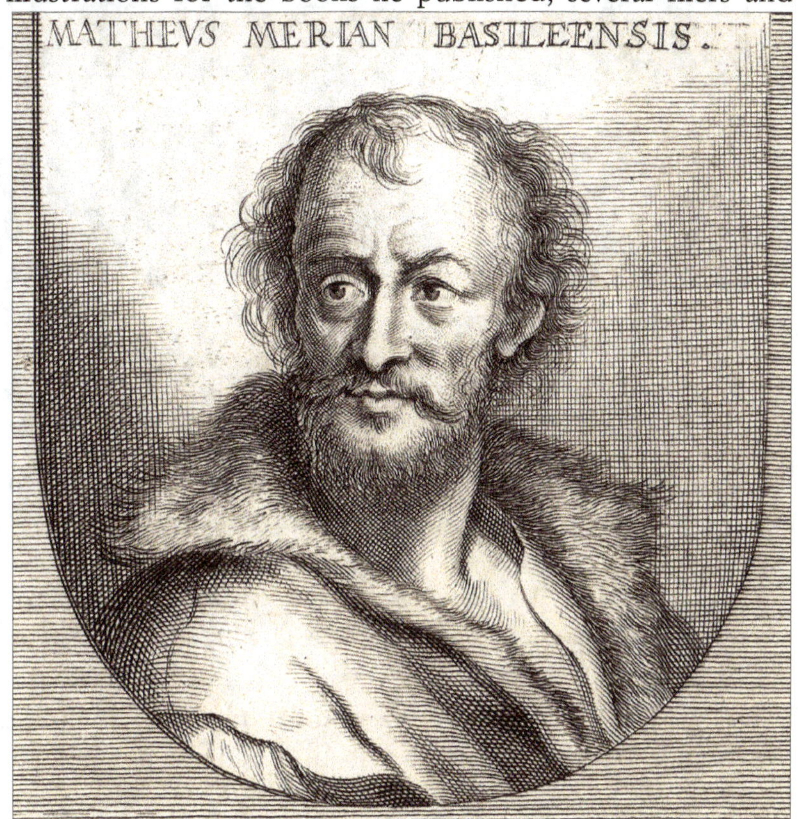

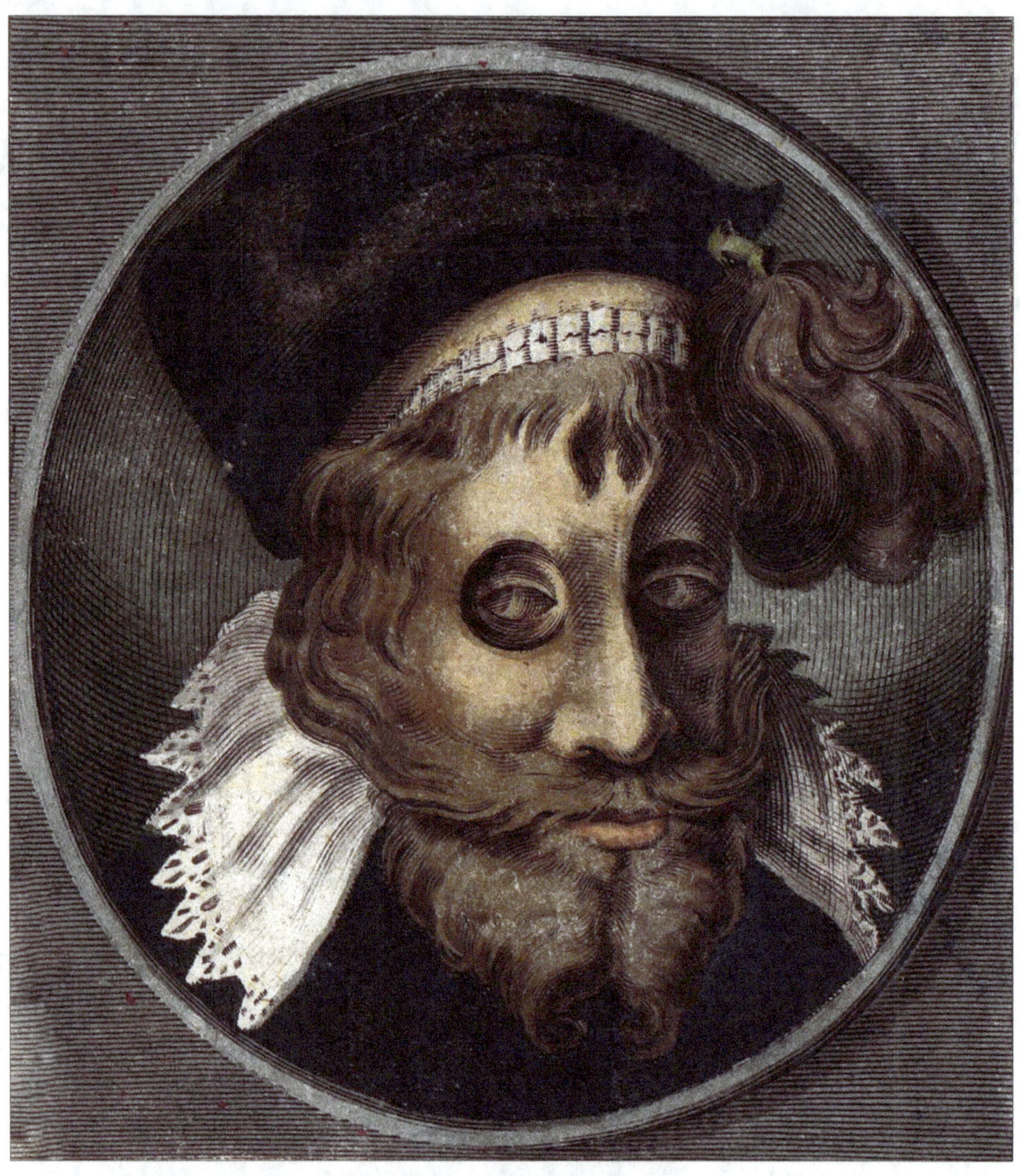

I thank thee, God. That I am not as other men are. Luke 18.
Thou sayest, I am rich and increased with goods, and do lack nothing. Revelation 3

Je ne suis point comme le reste des hommes. Luc, 18.
Tu dis: Je suis riche et Je suis dans l'abondance, et Je n'ai besoin de rien. Apocal, 3

Io non sono come tutti gli altri uomini. Luca, 18.
Tu dici: io sono ricco e vivo nell'abbondanza, e non ho bisogno di nulla.. Apocalisse 3

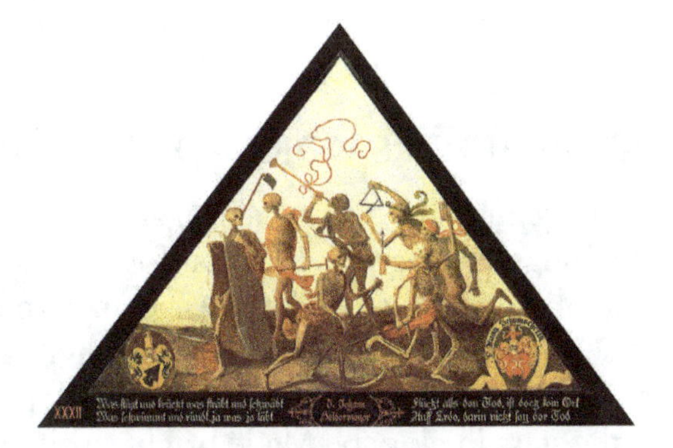

TODTEN TANZ

DEATH DANCE

DANCE DE LA MORT

DANZA DELLA MORTE

*

THE PLATES

THE PREACHERS WORD – Daniel, Ch 12

Many of those who sleep in dust, Shall wake again; God says, they must
Arise and at His Judgment seat receive what for their works is meet
Some life eternal, others grief And endless pain without relief.
Those who are wise shall brightly shine In heavenly light and joy divine;
And they, who many souls have taught , And wanderers back to God have brought,
Shall like the stars in glory be Made bright to all eternity.

*

LE PREDICATEUR, prenant pour texte Daniel, Chap. 12.

Lorsque l'ange de la vie Viendra dire aux trépassés
La promesse est accomplie Fils des hommes, paraissez !
Alors se levant en masse, On verra l'humaine race
Renaitre sur ses tombeaux Et d'un mouvement rapide
Avec l'ange qui la guide Transportée aux lieux très hauts
Là, sur un trône immutable Au milieu des Séraphins
Siège le juge équitable Promis à tous les humains
Il dit aux amés pieux Possédez mon Paradis !
Il dit aux amés rebelles Dans les flammes éternelles
Allez habiter, maudits !

*

IL PREDICATORE. Parola di Daniele c. 12

Molti di quelli che dormono nella polvere, dovranno svegliarsi di nuovo;
Dio dice, essi devono presentarsi al suo seggio del giudizio
dove riceveranno ciò che per le loro opere avranno meritato.
Alcuni la vita eterna, gli altri un dolore senza fine, senza sollievo.
Coloro che sono stati saggi, saranno accolti brillantemente
da una luce celeste e divina di gioia; e loro, che a molte anime hanno insegnato,
e molti pellegrini a Dio hanno portato,
Come le stelle in gloria, saranno luminosi per tutta l'eternità.

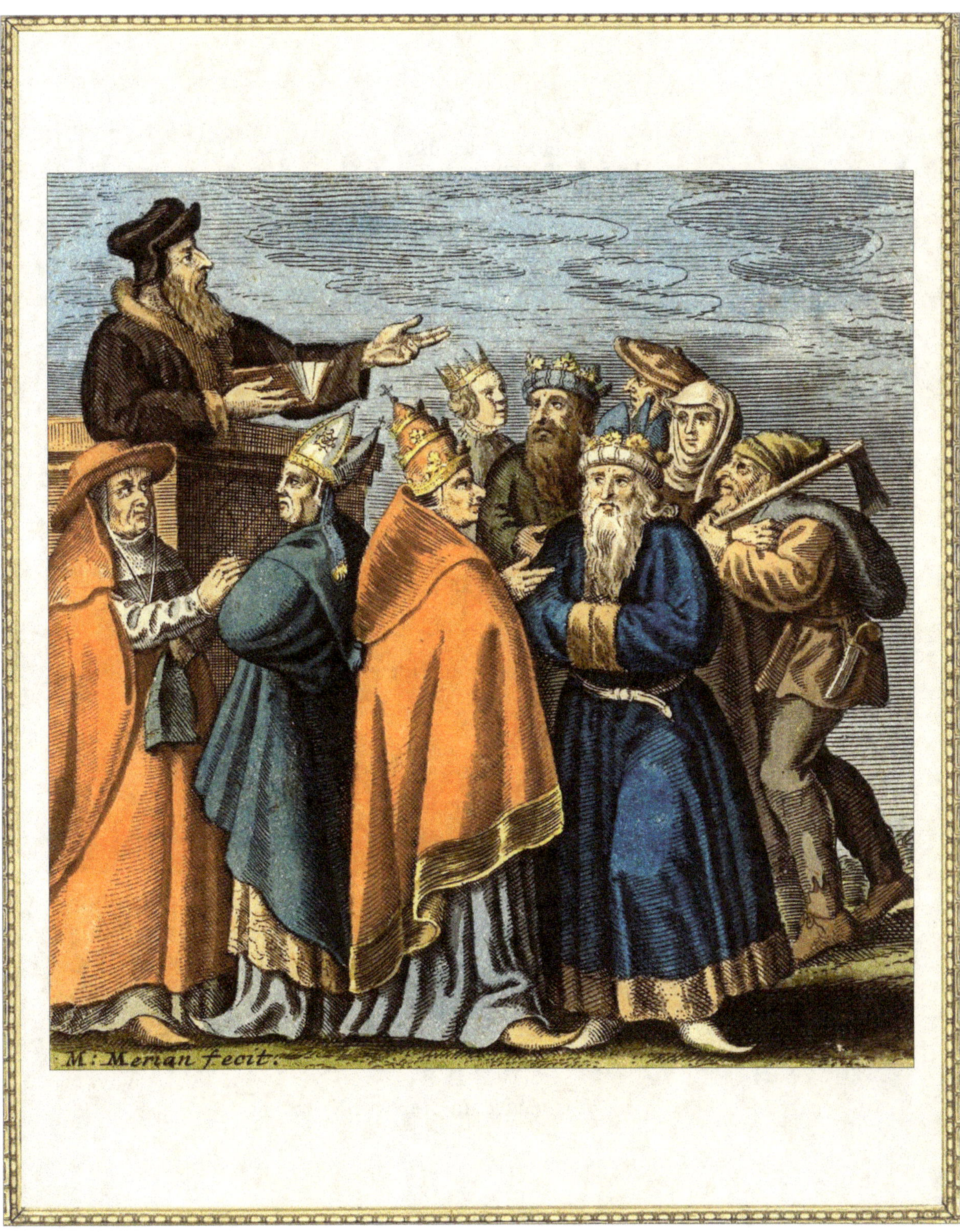
M: Merian fecit.

O man be wise,
Do not despise
The end designed
Of all mankind.
Such is thy fate
Early or late,
Like to the flower,
That lives an hour.

*

Mortel, avec respect contemple ta peinture:
Tels sont ces corps hideux, tel tu seas enfin;
Ainsi la fleur des champs qui fleurit au matin
Le soir n'est plus qu'un foin aride et sans figure.

*

O uomo saggio,
Non disprezzare
La fine è prevista
Per tutta l'umanità.
Tale è il tuo destino
Presto o tardi,
Come al fiore,
Che vive un'ora.

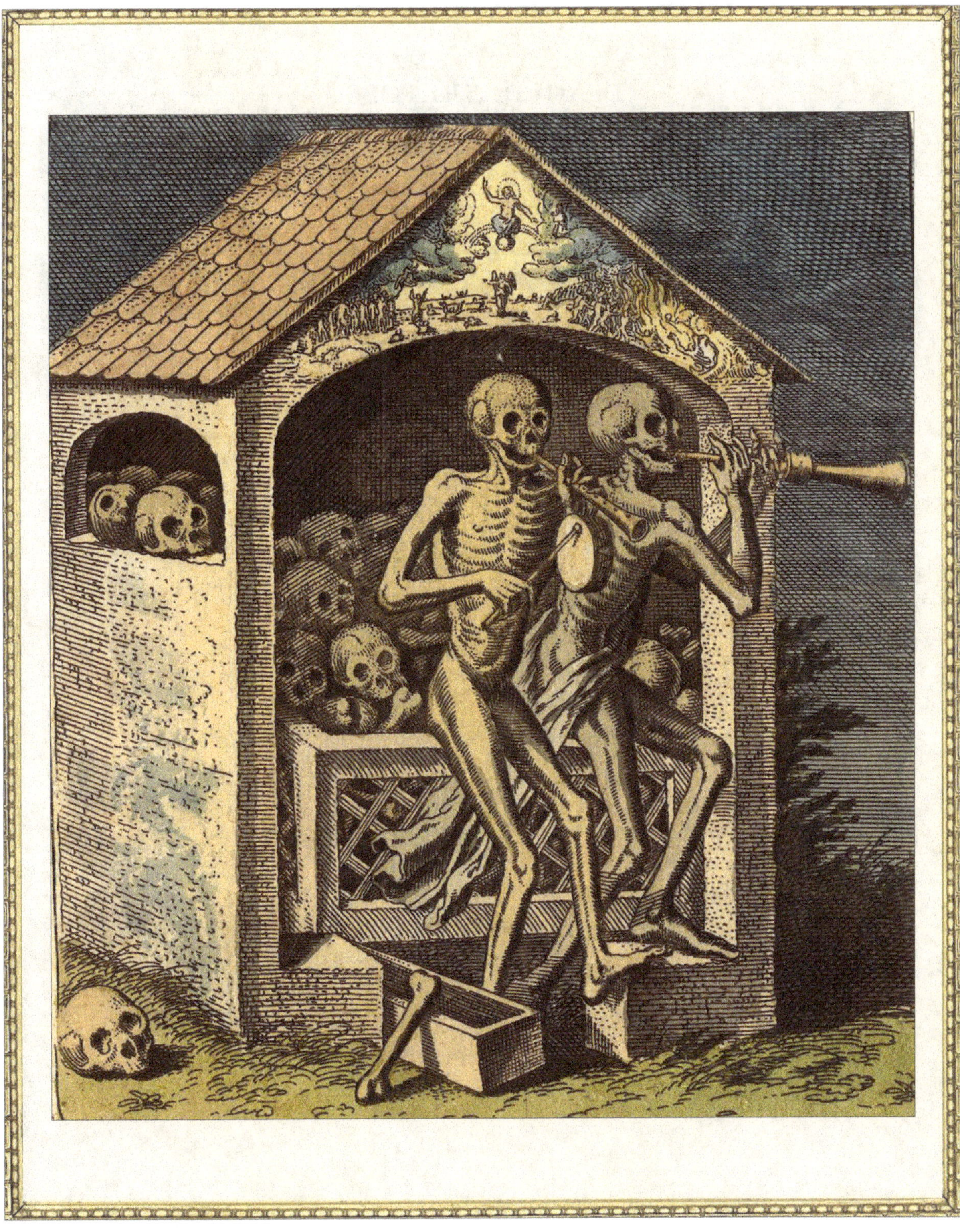

DEATH TO THE POPE
Come, holy father, you shall be the first to dance along with me !
Indulgence helps you not, lay down your double cross and tripple crown.

THE POPE'S REPLY
On earth my name was Holiness, next God mine was the highest place;
indulgence brought me wealth in store, but now death spares myself no more.

*

LA MORT AU PAPE

Saint-Pere, c'est à vous à commencer la danse
Je veux que le premier on vous voie avancer
Ni tiare, ni croix, ni le droit d'indulgence
De ce pas décisif ne peuvent dispenser.

RÉPONSE DU PAPE

Pontife indépendant et fier de ma puissance,
Régnant au nom de Dieu, je gouvernais sans lui;
Je vendais a haut prix des lettres de dispense..
Ah ! que ne peut la mort m'en vendre une aujourd'hui !

*

LA MORTE AL PAPA
Vieni, padre santo, tu sarai il primo a ballare con me!
L'indulgenza, la tiara e la doppia corona non ti dispenseranno.

RISPOSTA DEL PAPA
Sulla terra il mio nome era Santità, in nome di Dio regnavo da solo;
la vendita delle indulgenze mi ha portato molta ricchezza,
ma ora la morte non mi risparmia più...

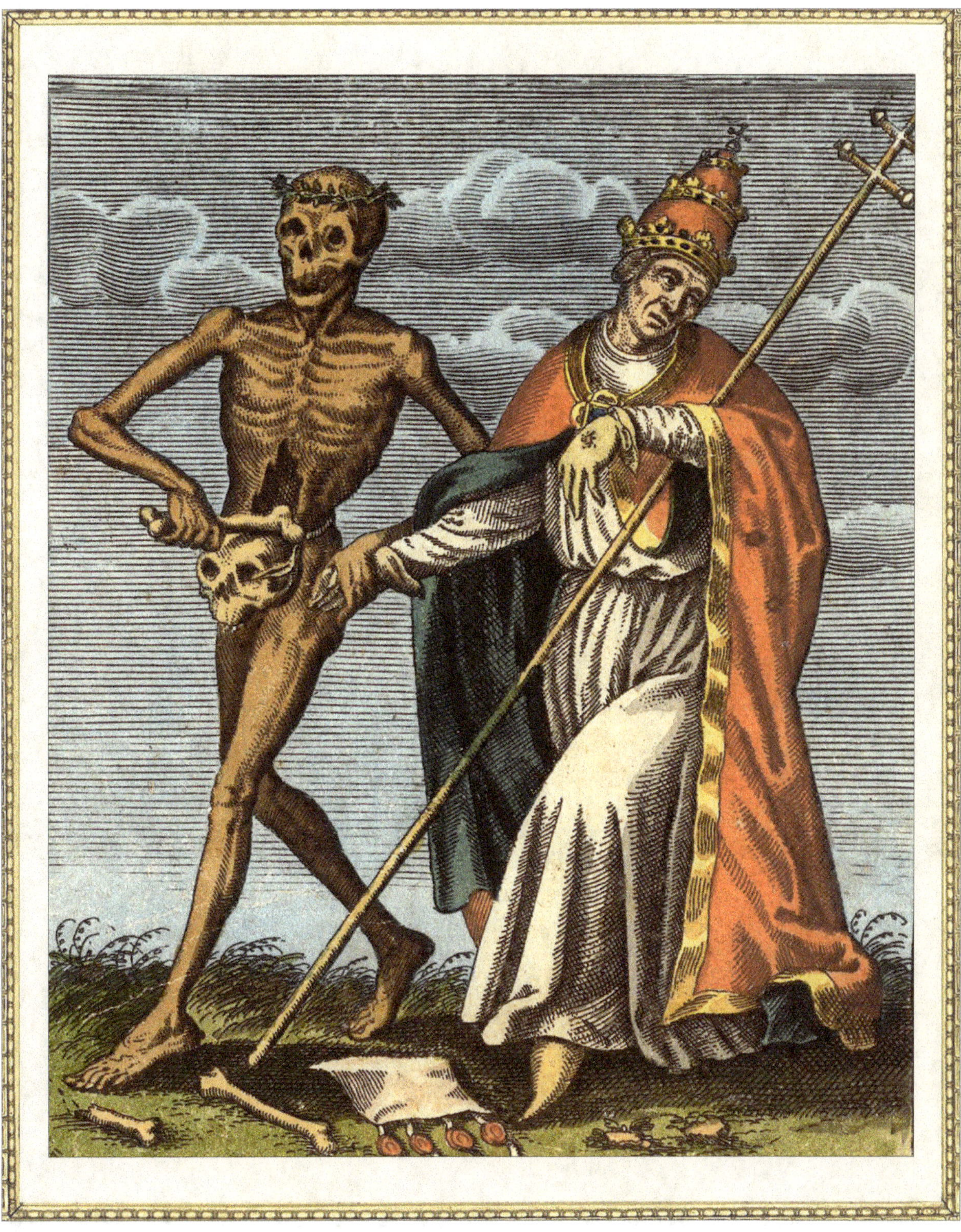

DEATH TO THE EMPEROR
Imperial Sire, your beard is grey. And still repentance finds delay;
'Tis vain to strive , you must go hence and to my doleful piping dance.

THE EMPEROR'S REPLY
My empire's bounds I could extend by force of arms the weak defend;
But death overcomes me in an hour, and leaves no trace of all my power.

*

LA MORT A L'EMPEREUR
Vous avez trop longtemps, Seigneur à barbe grise, ajourné votre repentir,
Allons, disposez vous: il n'est pIus de remise,
Et mon fifre discord vous invite à partir.

RÉPONSE DE L'EMPEREUR
Je pouvais, en héros, agrandir mon empire,
Protéger et venger l'humble à qui l'on fait tort;
Mais nu comble arrivé, tout mon pouvoir expire;
Suis-je encore Empereur? je ne suis plus qu'un mort.

*

LA MORTE ALL'IMPERATORE
Sire, la tua barba è grigia e, ahimè, la tua redenzione è in ritardo.
Smetti dunque di lottare, seguimi e danza a ritmo del mio flauto della discordia.

RISPOSTA DELL'IMPERATORE
Ho potuto estendere i confini del mio impero, lottando per difendere i più deboli;
ma la morte in un'ora o poco più spazza via tutto, senza lasciare
alcuna traccia del mio potere.

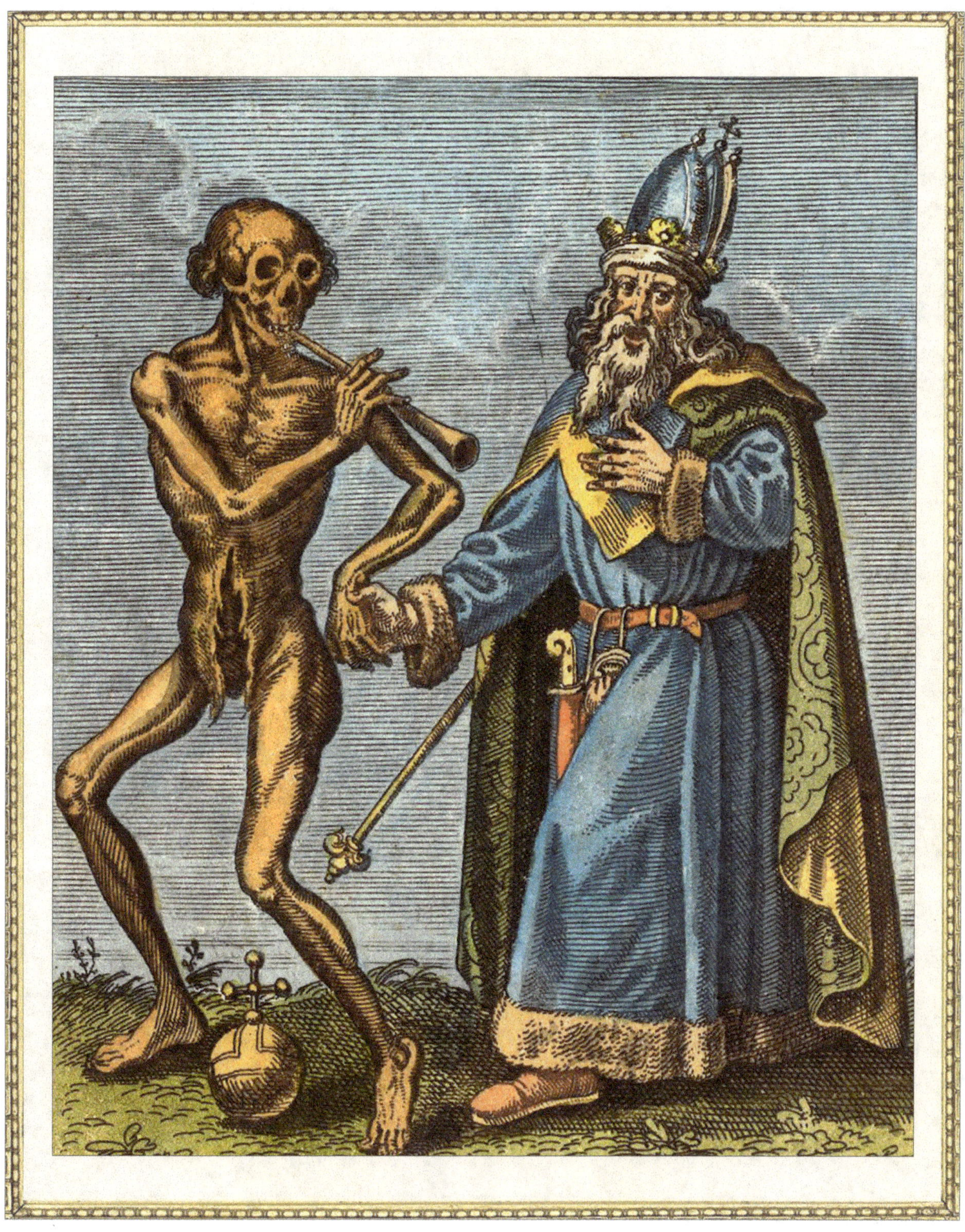

DEATH TO THE EMPRESS
Empress, for you I lead the way, the dance is mine, come quick, I pray;
Your ladies leave you all alone, and death now claims you as his own.

THE EMPRESS' REPLY
I've led a most luxurious life, because I was an Emperor's wife;
But now I'm forced to such a dance, all joy and gladness sink at once.

*

LA MORT A L'IMPERATRICE
Vos courtisans ont fui; nul d'entr'eux, ce me semble,
Ne s'approche de vous pour vous offrir la main:
Acceptez donc la mienne, et puis, dansons ensemble;
Mon bal a commencé, vous le mettrez en train.

RÉPONSE DE L'IMPERATRICE
J'ai passé tous mes juors au sein de la mollesse,
Femme d'un Empereur j'ai vécu pour jouir;
Puis la mort à son bal m'invite, elle me presse.
Je sens, à son aspect, tout mon coeur défaiIlir.

*

LA MORTE ALL'IMPERATRICE
Vieni altezza, ti faccio strada, coraggio. Le tue cortigiane ti hanno
lasciata tutta sola, ed ora la morte ti richiama a ballare al suo fianco

RISPOSTA DELL'IMPERATRICE
Ho vissuto una vitta lussuosa, poichè ero la moglie dell'Imperatore.
Ma ora la morte mi invita a questa danza macabra,
e tutta la gioia e la ricchezza svaniscono.

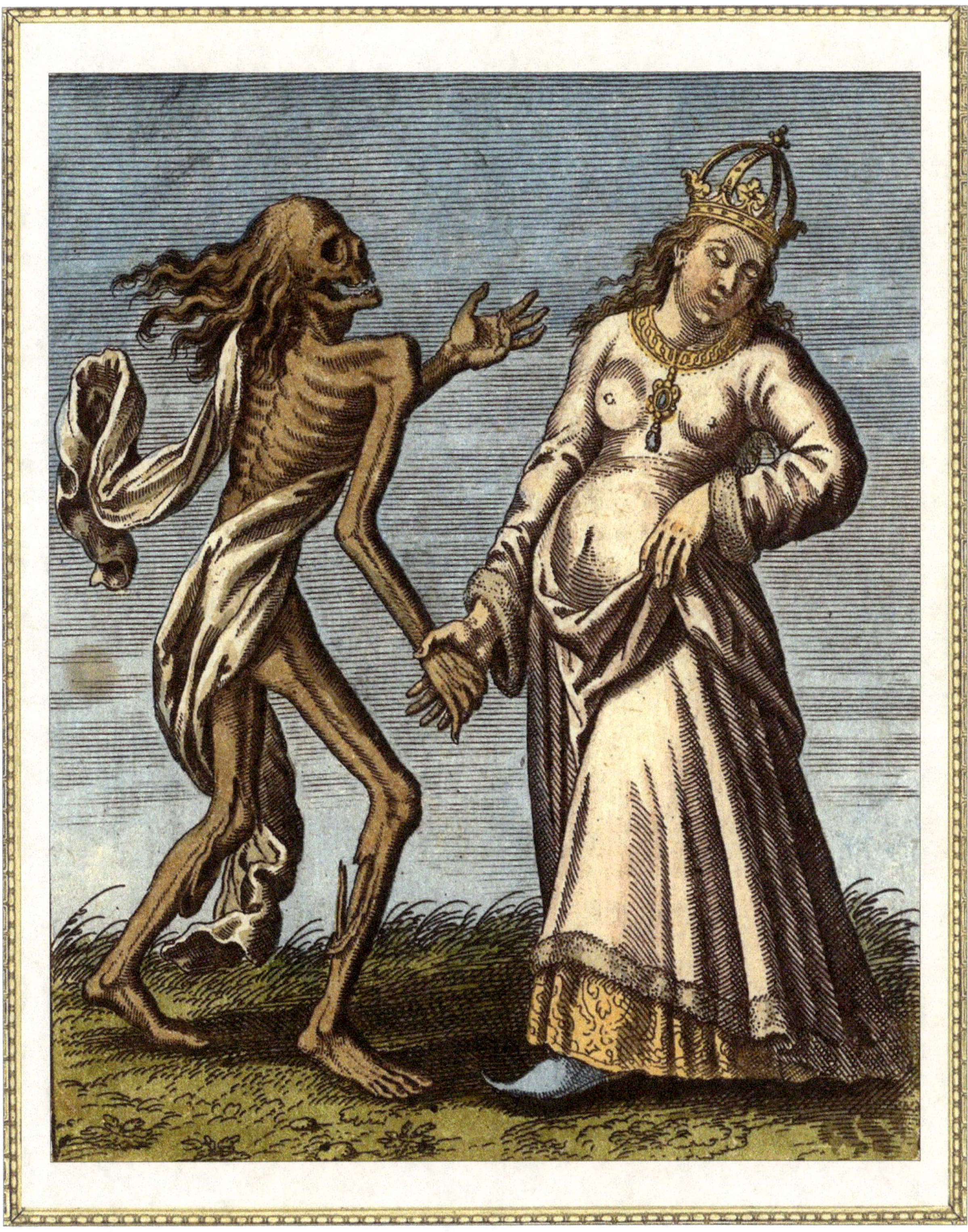

DEATH TO THE KING

Your power, o King, has ceased, my hand must lead you and my word command;
here all are brothers dry and bare, my diadem alone you'll wear.

THE KING'S REPLY

I lived in power and majesty; my throne was set in honour high;
yet now by death's strong hand I'm bound, his chains and cords my heart surround.

*

LA MORT AU ROI

Il n'est point ici-bas de puissance éternelle,
Sire Roi; venez donc, appuyé sur mon bras,
Venez vite grossir la bande fraternelle
Où, le front dépouillé, dansent les potentats.

RÉPONSE DU ROI

J'ai vécu redouté, puissant autant que brave.
Et sous mon joug d'airain haletait l'univers;
Il est libre à présent, et je deviens esclave;
De la puissante mort je vais porter les fers.

*

LA MORTE AL RE

Il tuo potere non esiste più, o Re.
Ora sei al comando della mia mano e della mia parola.
Vieni dai tuoi fratelli, secchi e spogli, indossando solo il mio diadema.

RISPOSTA DEL RE

Sono vissuto tra lo sfarzo ed il potere, il mio trono si ergeva sopra qualunque cosa.
Ma ora la mano della morte mi attanaglia;
le sue catene e corde circondano il mio cuore.

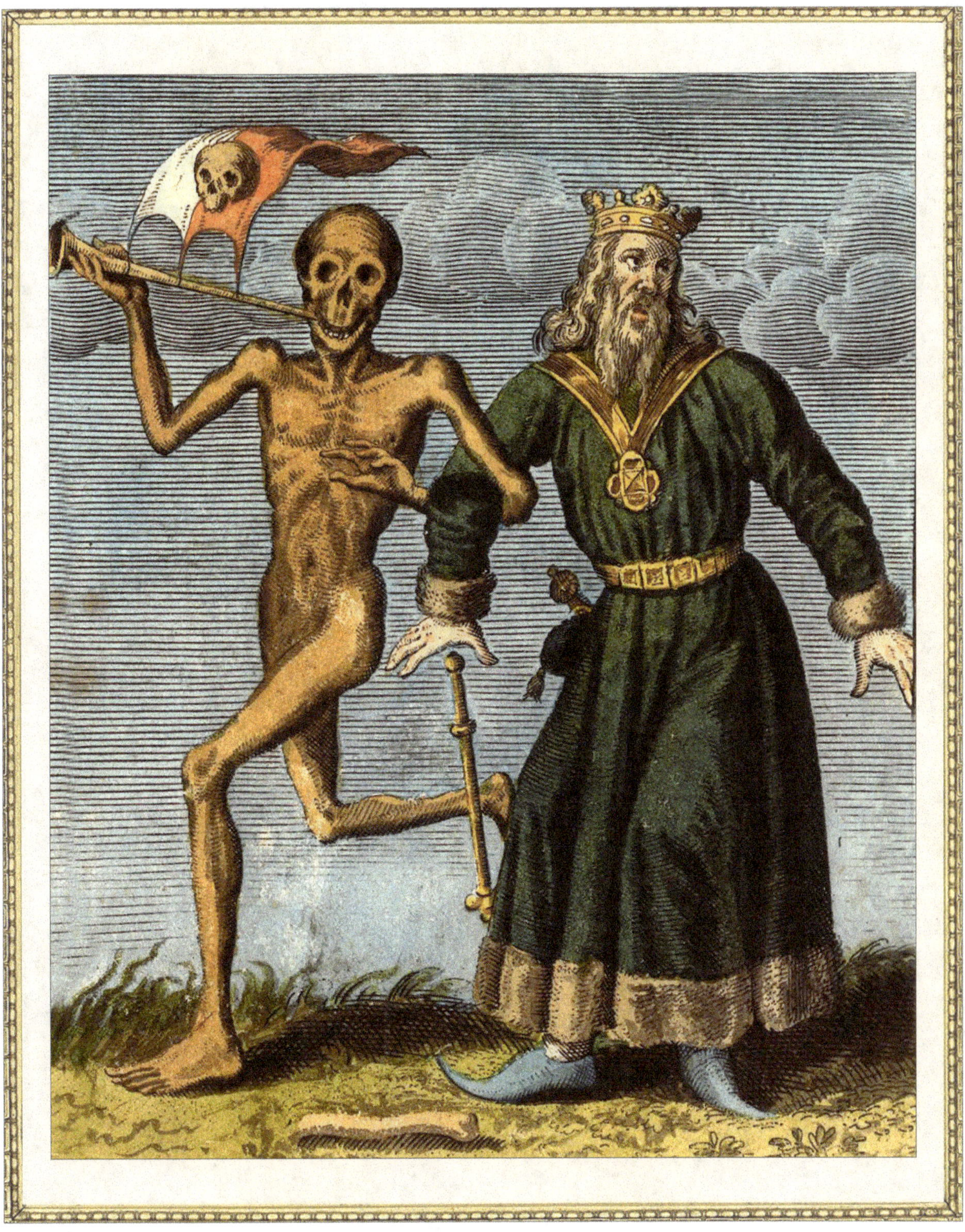

DEATH TO THE QUEEN

O Queen! For you there's no more room, you must descend into the tomb;
No gold avails nor beauty's sheen to keep you from the world unseen.

THE QUEEN'S REPLY

Alas! Alas! Now woe is me! Where are my maids? No one I see,
Of all with whom I used to smile; o Death! Yet spare me for a while.

*

LA MORT A LA REINE

Reine, le temps des jeux est passé sans retour;
Il faut m'accompagner dans les demeures sombres;
Vos attraits, vos joyaux et vos flatteurs de cour
Ne doivent point vous suivre au rendez-vous des ombres.

RÉPONSE DE LA REINE

Hélas! L'heure est venue, il faut quitter la vie ;
De tout ce que j'aimais il faut me départir;
O mort! Plus doucement, du repit, je t'en prie;
Laisse-moi vivre assez pour apprendre à mourir.

*

LA MORTE ALLA REGINA

O Regina! Nessuna stanza regale per te, devi scendere nella tua tomba.
Verranno con te tutti i tuoi gioielli, e la tua bellezza ormai passata.

RISPOSTA DELLA REGINA

Oh no! In che guaio mi sono cacciata! Dove sono le mie cameriere?
Non vedo nessuno, nessun viso familiare qui intorno.
O Morte! Risparmiami ancora un po'!

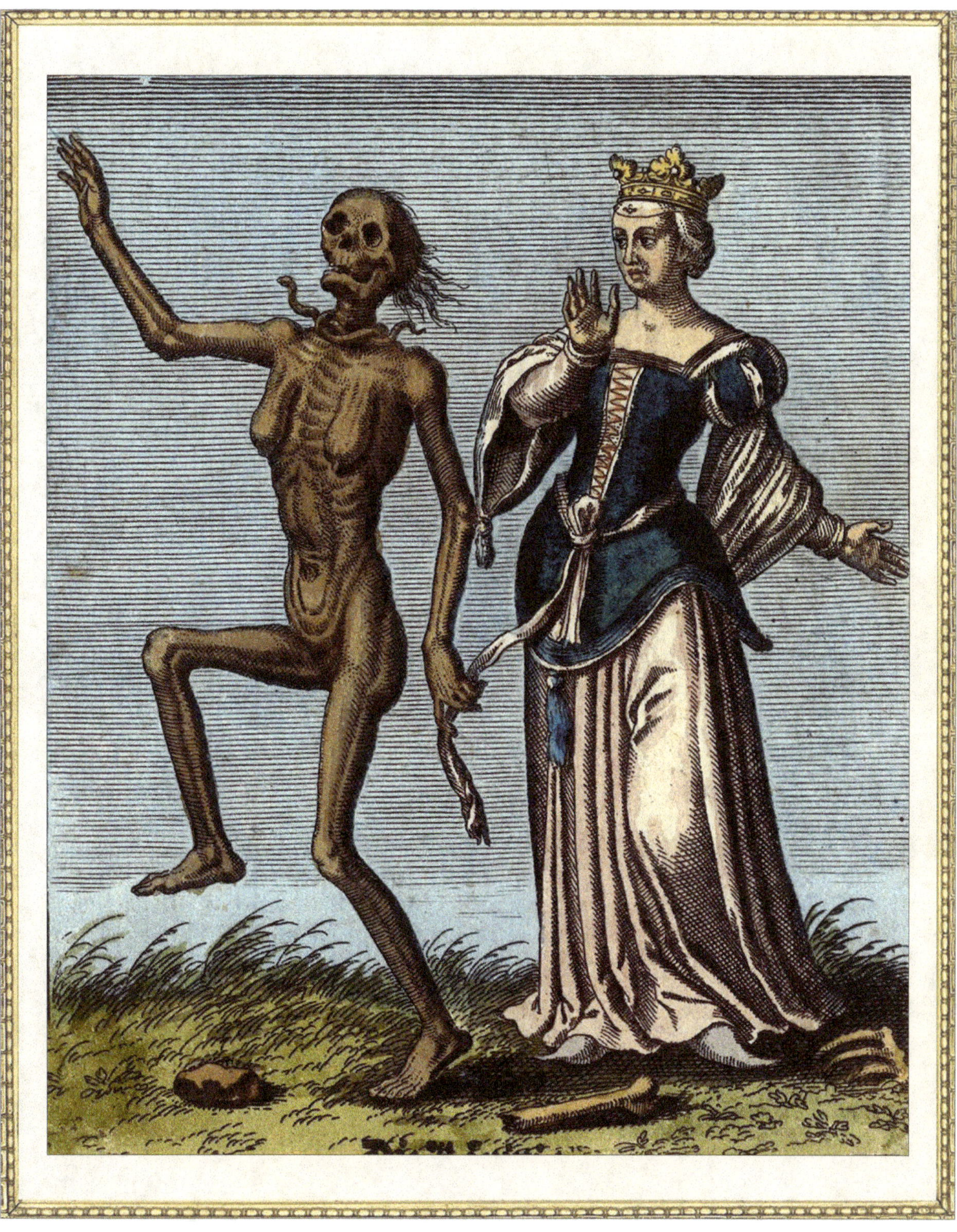

Die Königin

DEATH TO THE CARDINAL

Lord Cardinal, 'twill give me pleasure to see your red hat join the measure;
the laymen whom you oft have blest, are here and you must join the rest.

THE CARDINAL'S REPLY

A Cardinal, the Pope's own choice; the honour did my heart rejoice.
From men I could respect command, but death's dread power I can't withstand.

*

LA MORT AU CARDINAL

Votre barrette rouge eut des droits dans le monde;
Mais òu je vous conduis, chacun est votre égal;
Ceux que vos doigts levés bénissaient à la ronde
Vont danser avec vous, Monsieur le Cardinal.

RÉPONSE DU CARDINAL

Je devins Cardinal par le choix du saint-Père;
le monde sur ma tete entassa les honneurs.
N'importe, il faut mourir! Mourir, lorsque j'espère
monter en moins d'un an au faite des grandeurs.

*

LA MORTE AL CARDINALE

Eminenza, il tuo cappello rosso ti ha concesso privilegi in tutto il mondo.
Ma dove ti porto io, sono tutti uguali. I laici che avete battezzato sono riuniti qui,
ed è ora che tu li raggiunga.

RISPOSTA DEL CARDINALE

Sono diventato cardinale per scelta del Santo Padre, ed è stato un onore immenso.
Ho comandato con rispetto tanti uomini, ma non c'è nulla che possa fare contro il
potere della morte.

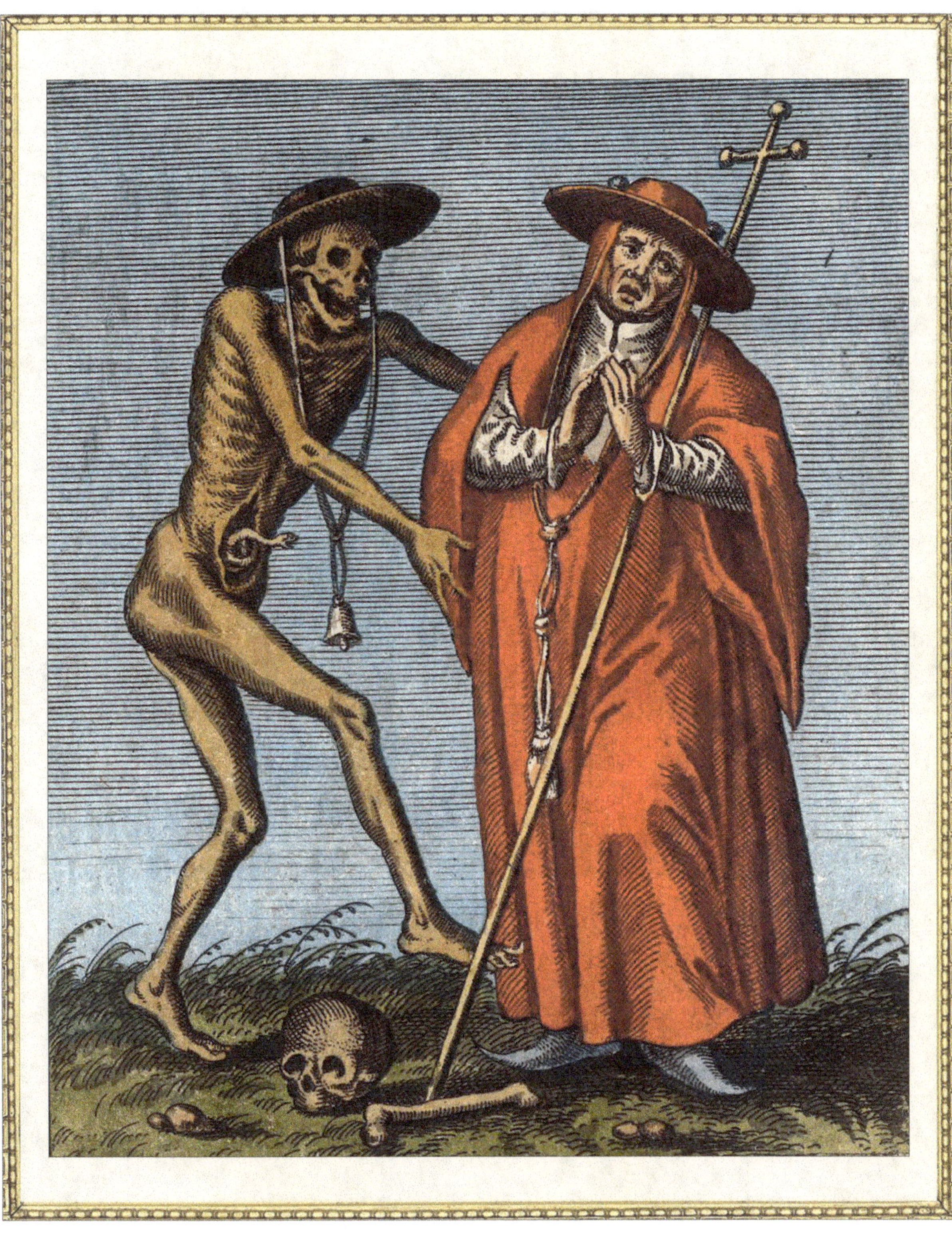

DEATH TO THE BISHOP

Bishop, your wisdom and your pride have turned your Reverence aside,
there where equality's the law, death's hand is ready you to draw.

THE BISHOP'S REPLY

The world admired and called me great because I held a Bishop's state;
now shapeless beings bear me off to where, like apes, they dance and scoff.

*

LA MORT A L'ÉVEQUE

En vain à mon pouvoir Votre Grandeur s'oppose;
a qui de mes arrets pourriez-vous appeler?
Allons, résignez-vous à la métamorphose:
au dernier de vos clercs vous allez ressembler.

RÉPONSE DE L'ÉVEQUE

Je portais, pléin d'orgueil, la crosse épiscopale,
ma gravité sévère imposait aux humains;
terrible changement! Une troupe infernale
fair danser comme un fou l'égal des souverains.

*

LA MORTE AL VESCOVO

La tua saggezza e il tuo orgoglio si oppongono invano al mio potere, Vescovo.
Rassegnati alla metamorfosi: diverrai uguale a tutti gli altri uomini.

RISPOSTA DEL VESCOVO

Il mondo mi ha ammirato e acclamato, perché avevo il titolo di Vescovo.
Ora degli esseri informi come bestie mi invitano a ballare
una danza infernale.

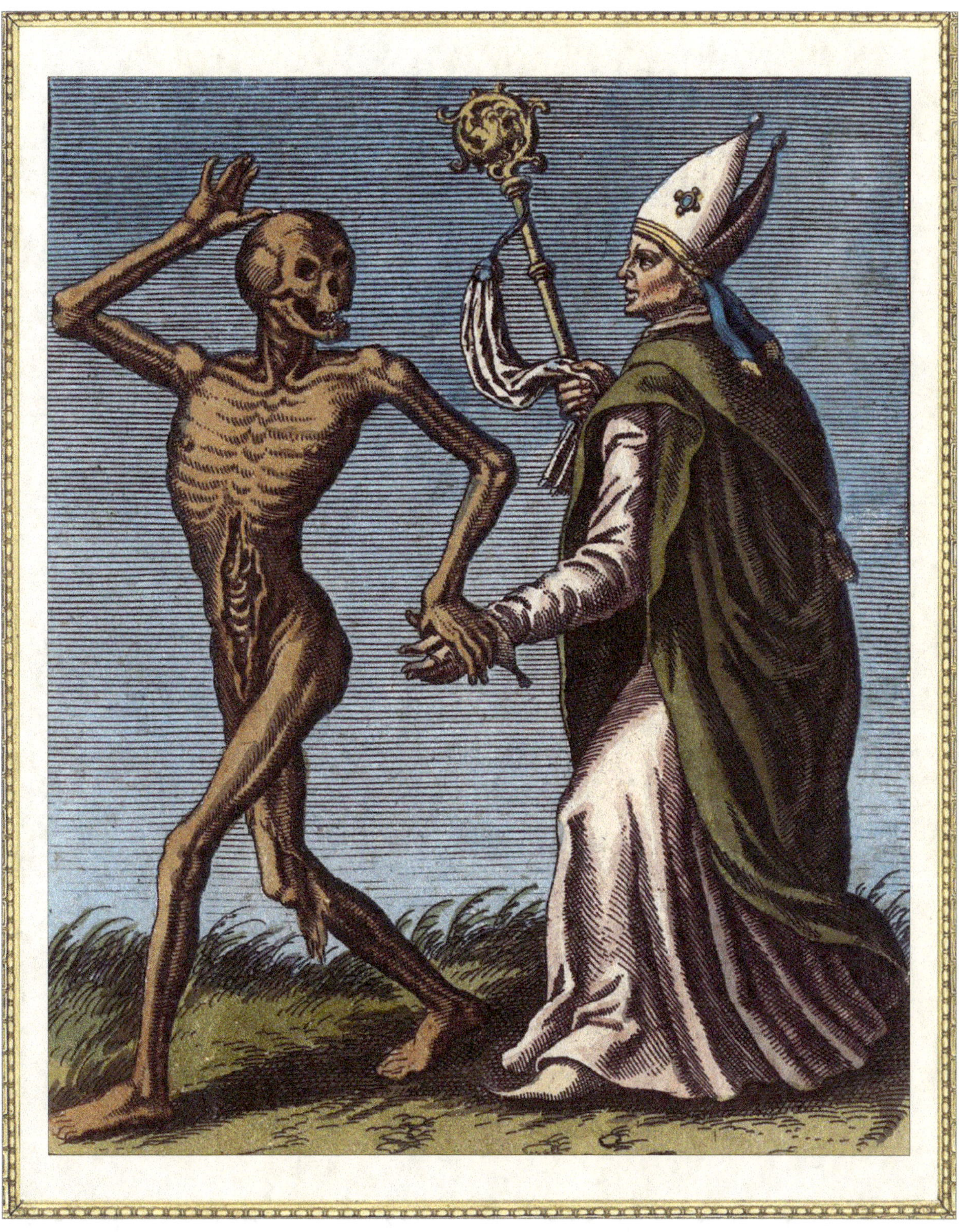

DEATH TO THE DUKE
With ladies you have long danced well, proud Duke, and of success can tell;
for this you'll pay the forfeit meet, be pleased now the dead to greet.

THE DUKE'S REPLY
Woe's me! Must I with haste so wild leave land and followers, wife and child?
God in his kingdom pity me, since I must like my dancer be.

*

LA MORT AU DUC
Les belles vous aimaient; dans leurs danses légères,
dans leurs folatres jeux qui brillait plus que vous?
Venez d'un autre bal connaitre les mystéres;
les objets de vos feux un jour y seront tous.

RÉPONSE DU DUC
Faut-il sitot quitter biens, dignités, patrie,
ma femme et mes enfants,
pour m'en aller danser en sotte compagnie?
Dieu m'aide! Sots pour sots, j'aimais mieux les vivants.

*

LA MORTE AL DUCA
Nella tua vita hai incontrato molte donzelle, e hai danzato con loro, o Duca.
Ma tutto nella vita ha un prezzo: ora preparati ad incontrare la morte.

RISPOSTA DEL DUCA
Povero me! Devo salutare di corsa i miei seguaci, mia moglie e mio figlio?
Che Dio mi perdoni, devo ballare con la morte in persona.

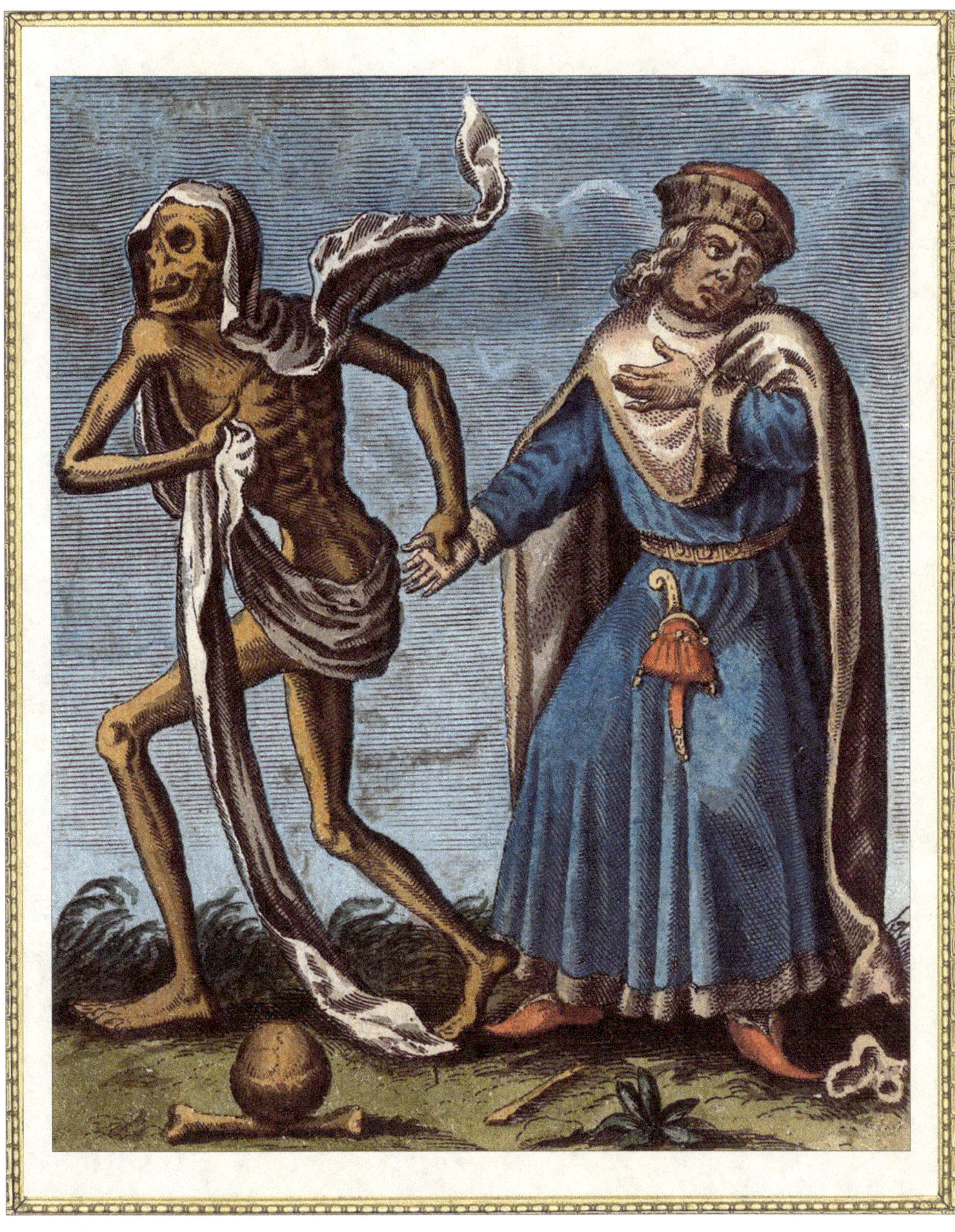

DEATH TO THE DUCHESS
All hail! My lady Duchess fine, altho' you're of a noble line,
and high respect have long had here, yet still to me you're no less dear.

THE DUCHESS' REPLY
My poor lute's well known sound I know, heavens! With this monster must I go?
Short time I've been a Duchess gay, and now I must die! Oh! Lack-a-day!

*

LA MORT A LA DUCHESSE
Noble sang, noble coeur, et beauté sans seconde,
que de justes raisons de se louer du sort!
Et pourtant vous mourrez; car ce qui plait au monde,
ne déplut jamais à la mort.

RÉPONSE DE LA DUCHESSE
Ce monstre, dont la main ose outrage la lyre,
quoi! C'est lui qui me sert de page et d'écuyer!
Duchesse hier, des rois ont brigué mon sourire...
Aujourd'hui ce fantome est mon seul chevalier.

*

LA MORTE ALLA DUCHESSA
Salve Duchessa! Grazie alla tua nobile linea di sangue, sei stata onorata e rispettata
da tutti, in vita. Sappi che per me questo non fa alcuna differenza.

RISPOSTA DELLA DUCHESSA
Questo mostro osa impugnare la così bella lira! Che disgrazia! Solo ieri ero una
Duchessa felice, e i re si contendevano il mio sorriso.
Ora mi rimane solo questo cavaliere fantasma.

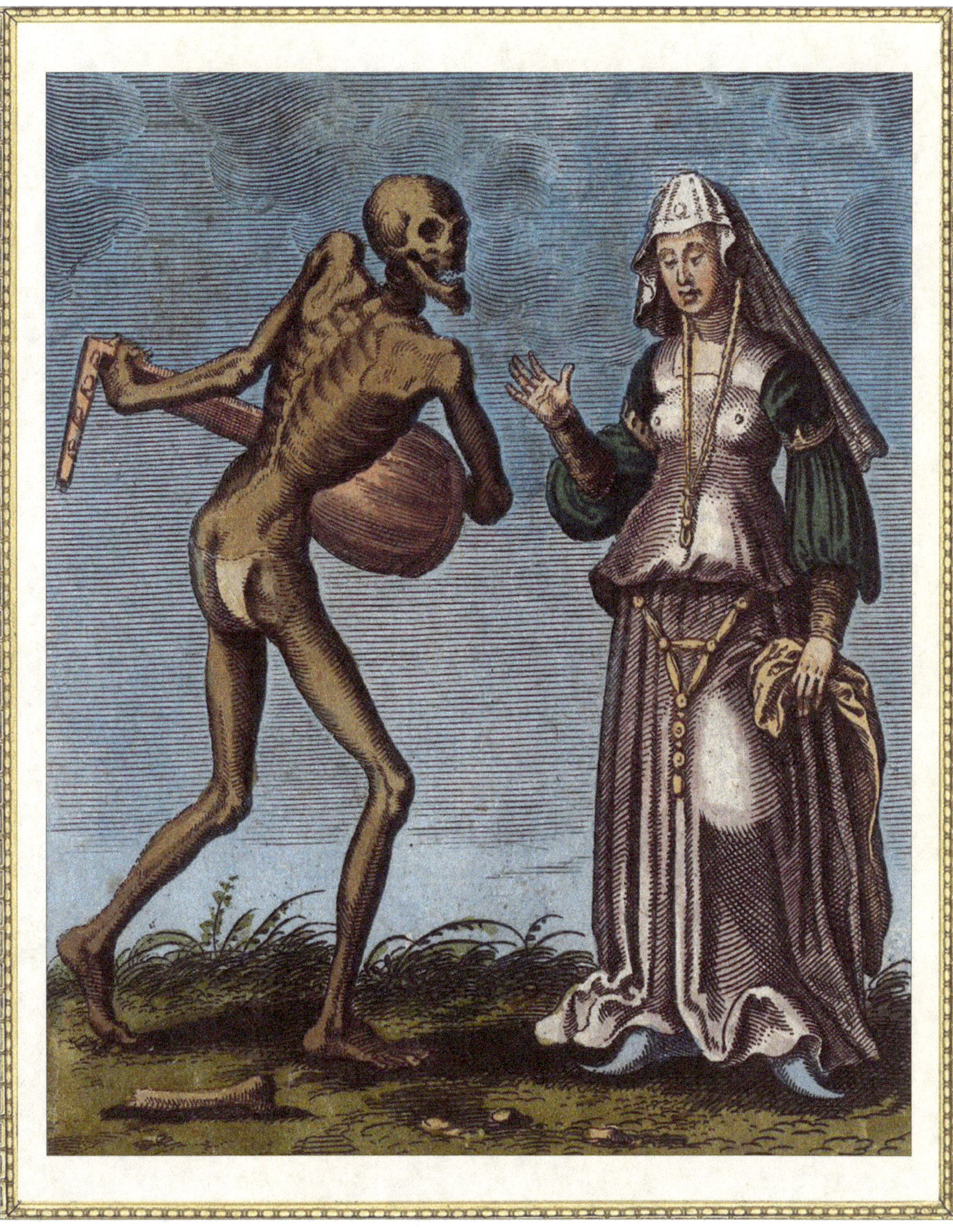

DEATH TO THE EARL

Sir Earl, give me the runner's fee, most bitter news Death brings to thee;
for wife and child do not complain, you now must dance with vulgar men.

THE EARL' S REPLY

Throughout the world I was well famed and noble Earl was always named,
now Death has struck me down at once and borne me off to join his dance.

*

LA MORT AU COMTE

Comte, je vous annonce une étrange disgrace:
il faut venir danser où dansent vos vassaux,
que sert de rappeler l'éclat de votre race?
La bas tout est roture, et les morts sont égaux.

RÉPONSE DU COMTE

"Noble Comte" me dit le vassal qui s'incline,
mon nom est répandu, les livres en sont pleins;
mais le Comte, en dépit de sa noble origine,
vilain, ira danser avec d'autres vilains.

*

LA MORTE AL CONTE

Ebbene Conte, temo di non avere buona notizie per te: devi venire a danzare con i
vassalli, gli stessi che prima ti servivano. Ti svelo un segreto:
da morti siete tutti uguali.

RISPOSTA DEL CONTE

I vassalli si inchinavano a me, chiamandomi "nobile Conte"; il mio nome risplende
sui libri, ma oggi le mie nobili origine non mi salveranno:
ballerò con gli altri villani.

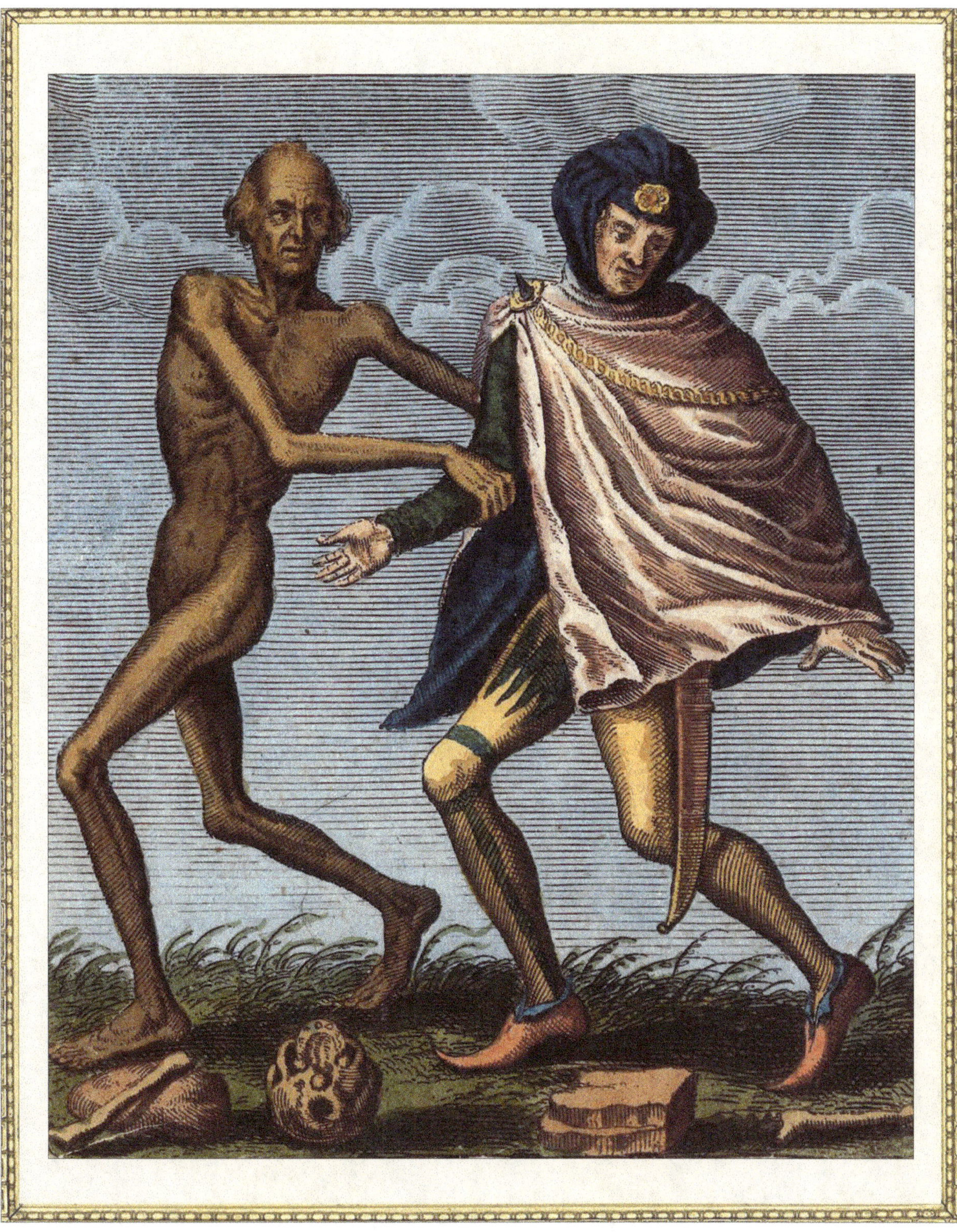

DEATH TO THE ABBOT

Abbot, your mitre I must loose, your staff is now of no more use;
if here you've been a shepherd true, high honour is prepared for you.

THE ABBOT'S REPLY

I rose to Abbot's high estate and long enjoy'd my honours great;
none dared resist my high behest, and yet Death makes me like the rest.

*

LA MORT A L'ABBÉ

Sire Abbé, dépouillez cette riche parure;
si vous avez fidèlement
a tout votre troupeau donné la nourriture,
son salut dans le ciel sera votre ornement.

RÉPONSE DE L'ABBÉ

En véritable Abbé j'ai vécu, je l'espère;
grossissant de mon mieux le trésor du couvent;
sévère sur mes droits, du reste bon vivant:
pourquoi done m'interrompre en train de si bien faire?

*

LA MORTE ALL'ABATE

Abate, spogliati dai tuoi ricchi ornamenti; se è vero che hai fedelmente nutrito e
servito il tuo gregge, il tuo nuovo ornamento sarà la salvezza nei cieli.

RISPOSTA DELL'ABATE

Sono stato un buon Abate, Dio mi è testimone: ho fatto del mio meglio per
proteggere i tesori del convento, sono stato severo ma giusto.
Per quale motivo, morte, mi fermi proprio ora?

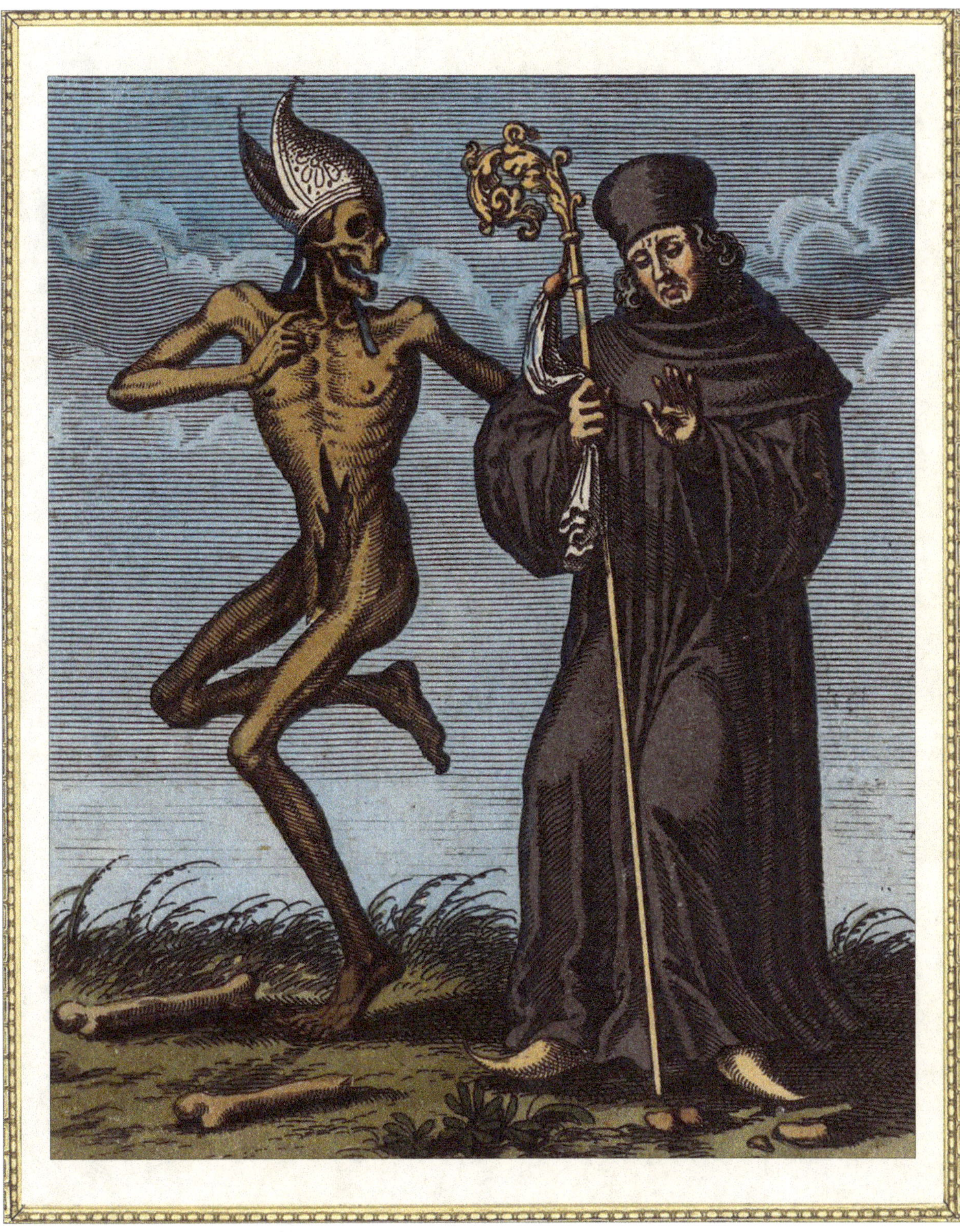

DEATH TO THE KNIGHT

Sir Knight, your name is in my list. From fighting you could not desist,
but when you must with Death contend, your power and skill are at an end.

THE KNIGHT'S REPLY

As true and valiant Knight I've served the world, and ne'er from duty swerved;
but now against all Knighthood's law does Death to his dread dance me draw.

*

LA MORT AU CHEVALIER

Les morts m'ont reconté votre insigne vaillance;
vos exploits éclatants ont peuplé mes états;
mais sur moi vainement vous lèveriez la lance:
car quel est le vainqueur que je ne vaincrais pas?

RÉPONSE DU CHEVALIER

Modèle de nos preux, appui de la patrie,
des opprimés le reconfort,
de l'ordre de chevalerie
je me vois dégradé par les mains de la mort.

*

LA MORTE AL CAVALIERE

Sembra che il tuo nome sia sulla mia lista, Cavaliere. Proprio tu, che non potevi
esimerti dai combattimenti, sei giunto al tuo scontro finale, con me.

RISPOSTA DEL CAVALIERE

Ho servito lealmente il mondo e la mia patria, sotto l'ordine dei Cavalieri;
ora nessun ordine e nessuna legge possono salvarmi dall'incontro con la morte.

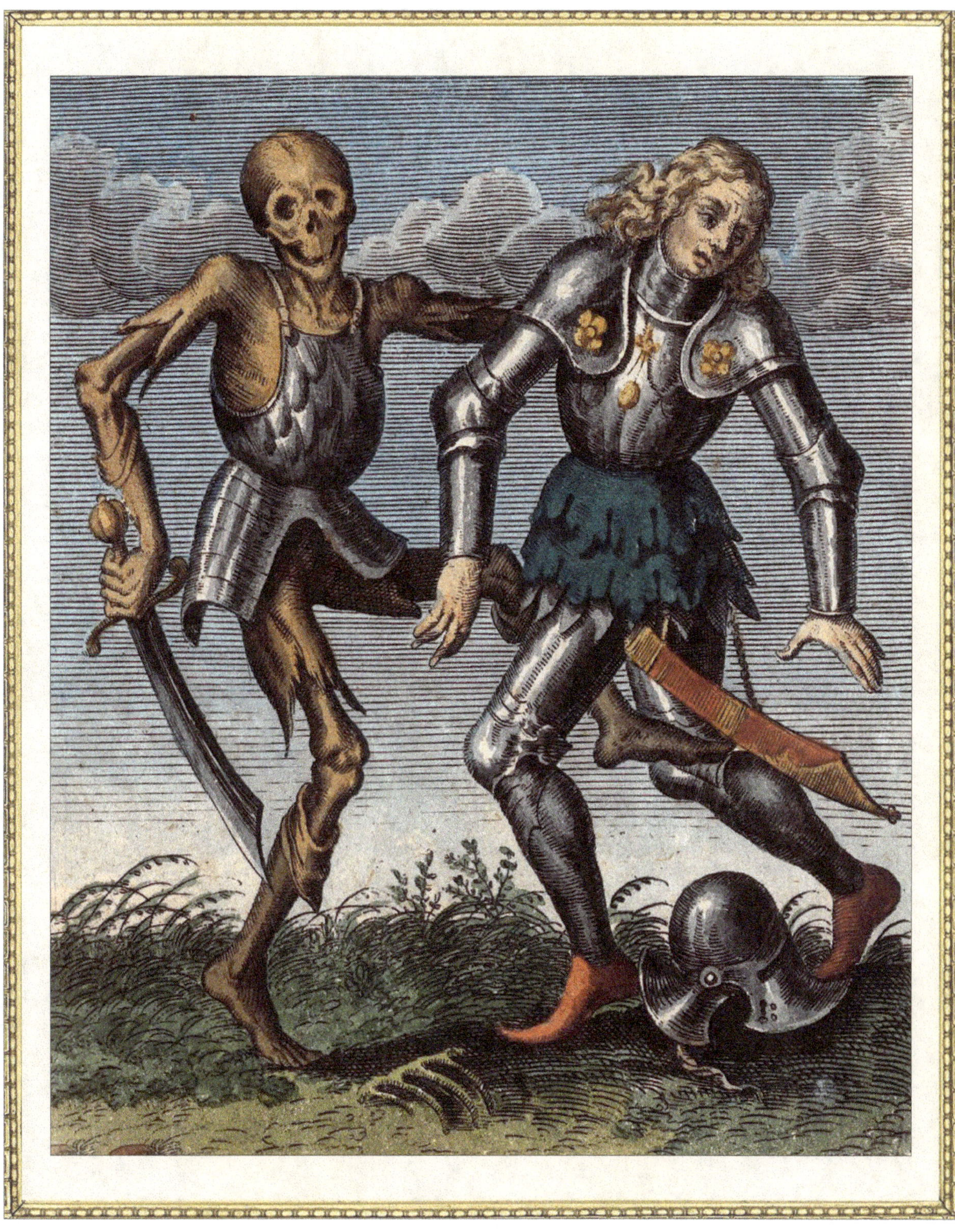

DEATH TO THE LAWYER

No dodge helps now, no courtly phrase, protest, appeal, nor law's delays,
death lays arrest on every class, clerk and civilian, none can pass.

THE LAWYER'S REPLY

From God all law and truth proceed, as in the books each one may read;
to warp these should no lawyer try, but love the truth and hate the lie.

*

LA MORT AU JURISCONSULTE

Cherchez dans les détours de la jurisprudence
s'il est quelque secret pour éluder mes loix
l'arret est sans appel; vous viendrez à ma dance:
de plus savants que vous ont reconnu mes droits.

RÉPONSE DU JURISCONSULTE

C'est de moi seul, dit Dieu, que vient toute justice,
inflexible au méchant, à l'opprimé propice;
le juge sur ma loi toujours se règlera.
L'ai-je fait? Dieu le sait, Dieu me jugera.

*

LA MORTE ALL'AVVOCATO

Prova a controllare se nei tuoi libri e nelle tue leggi c'è un qualche segreto
per eludere le mie; altrimenti la mia sentenza è definitiva: il punto d'arrivo
è la danza con me.

RISPOSTA DELL'AVVOCATO

Dice Dio che la verità e la giustizia passano da me. Sono inflessibile con i malvagi, ed
equamente ho sempre cercato la giustizia. Solo Dio mi giudicherà.

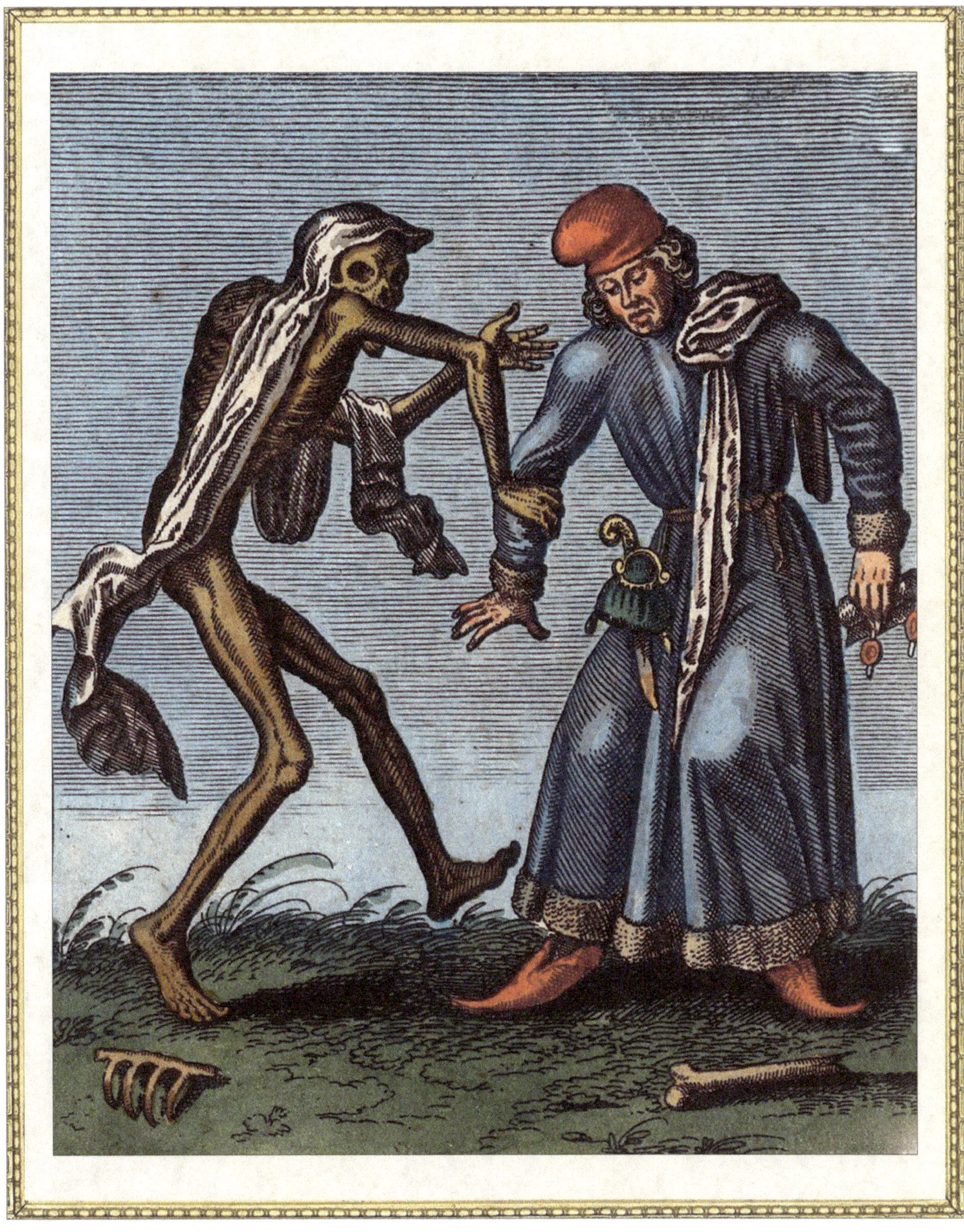

DEATH TO THE ALDERMAN
Have you been long a city-lord and had your seat at council board?
And giv'n good judgement? Well's your hap! Still I must now remove your cap.

THE ALDERMAN'S REPLY
Both day and night I've laboured much that none the common good might touch;
of rich and poor the welfare sought, and still the best to pass I brought.

*

LA MORT AU MAGISTRAT
Je viens te dépouiller...mais au magistrat sage
qui fit régner la loi, proscrivit les abus,
la mort peut enlever, à titre de péage,
sa toge et ses honneurs, et non pas ses vertus.

RÉPONSE DU MAGISTRAT
La publique félicité
fut l'object de mes soins, ma principale affaire;
j'ai fait ce que j'ai pu, la divine bonté
rendra compte à chacun du bien qu'il voulut faire.

*

LA MORTE AL MAGISTRATO
Vengo a scuoiarti...ma a te, saggio Magistrato, che hai fatto regnare la legge e
denunciato gli abusi, posso togliere tutto, non le virtù.

RISPOSTA DEL MAGISTRATO
Il benessere del popolo è sempre stato il mio obiettivo principale,
il mio scopo nella vita, e credo di aver fatto del mio meglio.
La divina bontà giudica le azioni di ognuno di noi.

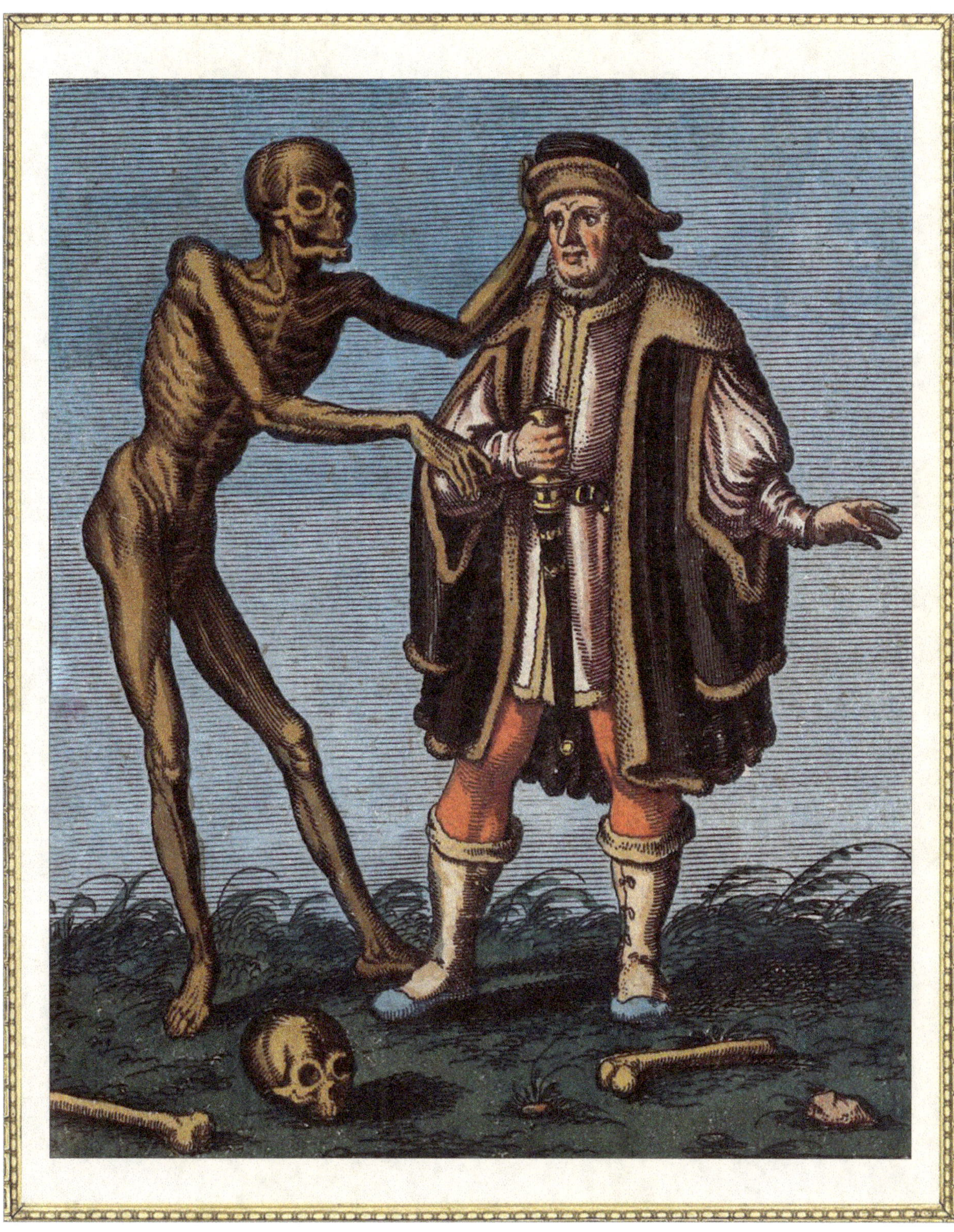

DEATH TO THE CANON

So, Canon, you have loud and long been chaunting out your choral song;
now harken to my pipe so clear, announcing that your death is here.

THE CANON'S REPLY

Yes, I have sung as canon free, full many a grave sweet melody;
but death's pipe such discord has made, that I'm sore startled and afraid.

*

LA MORT AU CHANOINE

De sons harmonieux son oreille nourrie
espère encore gouter d'agreables accords;
mais de mon sifflet entend les sons discords:
ce sera désormais ta seule mélodie.

RÉPONSE DU CHANOINE

Jour et nuit mes chants la grave mélodie
remplissait le saint lieu du nom du Roi des Roi;
la mort va terminer mes chants avec ma vie,
et son aigre sifflet déja couvre ma voix.

*

LA MORTE AL CANONICO

Canonico, so che hai cantato più e più volte le tue canzoni corali;
ora vorrei che gridassi nel mio corno che è giunta la tua ora.

RISPOSTA DEL CANONICO

Sì, ho cantato liberamente e composto armoniose melodie;
ma il corno della morte è così stridente che sono spaventato ed impaurito.

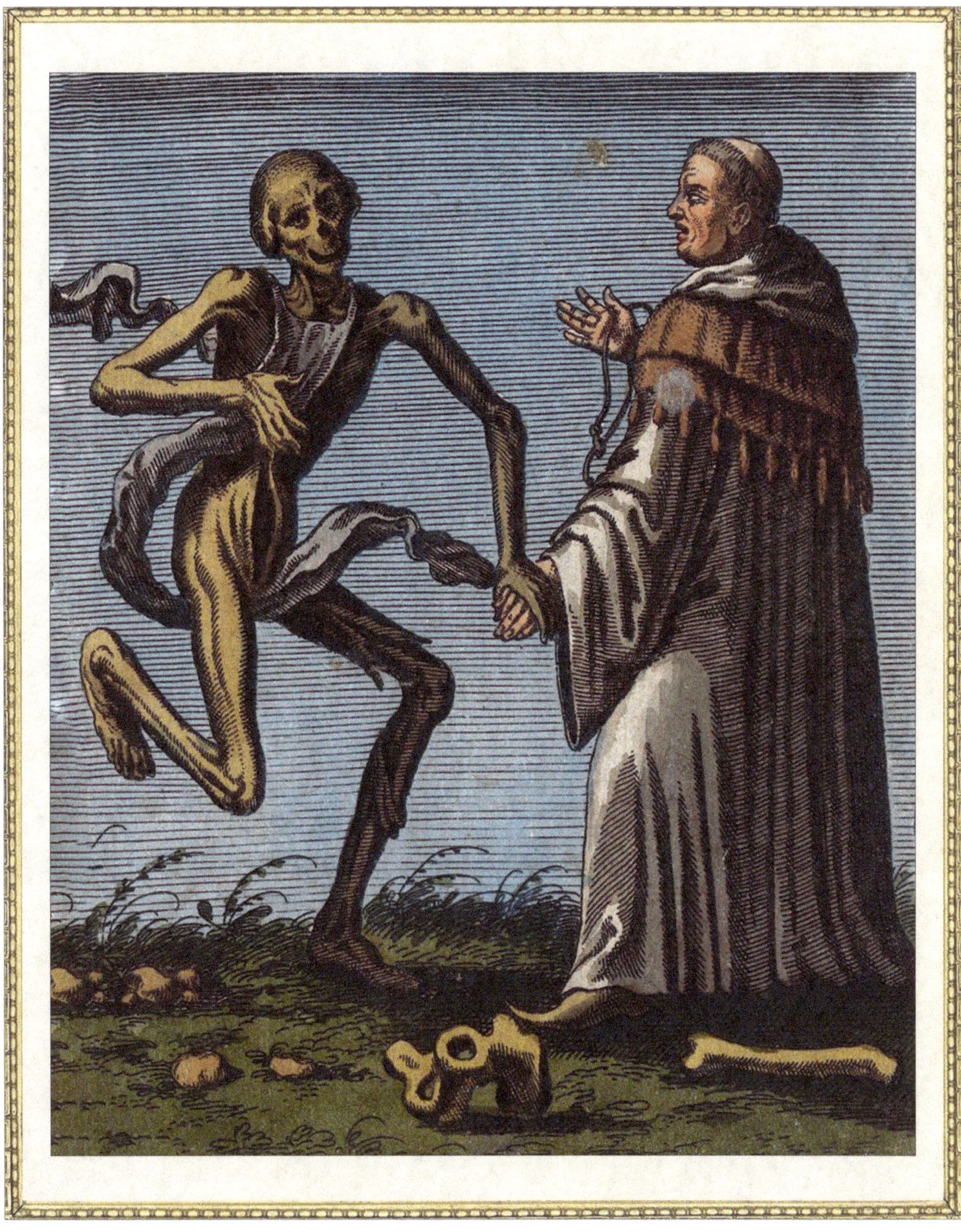

DEATH TO THE DOCTOR
Doctor! Look at my skeleton and tell me if it's all well done;
many have been dispatch's by thee who all do now resemble me.

THE DOCTOR'S REPLY
Thro' skill in water long renown'd, Ive help for man and woman found;
but who will mine inspect, I pray? Now that Death calls myself away.

*

LA MORT AU MÉDECIN
Des morts, dont vos talents ont peuplé mon empire,
mon squelette mouvant vous offre tous les traits;
leur corps de corps humain vous apprit les secrets:
quelque jour sur le votre on pourra s'en instruire.

RÉPONSE DU MÉDECIN
Les deux sexes chez moi venaient avec mystère
m'apporter certaine eau qui m'apprenait leur mal;
qui voudra voi la mienne, en me tirer d'affaire?
Hélas! Il est trop tard: voici l'instant fatal.

*

LA MORTE AL MEDICO
Dei morti, che popolano il mio impero, il mio scheletro mobile vi offre tutti i tratti.
I corpi umani sono stati la tua scuola, Medico: ora qualcuno potrà imparare sul tuo.

RISPOSTA DEL MEDICO
Ho aiutato uomini e donne a stare meglio e a curare la loro salute,
ma chi verrà in aiuto a me stavolta? Ahimè nessuno: è giunta l'ora fatale.

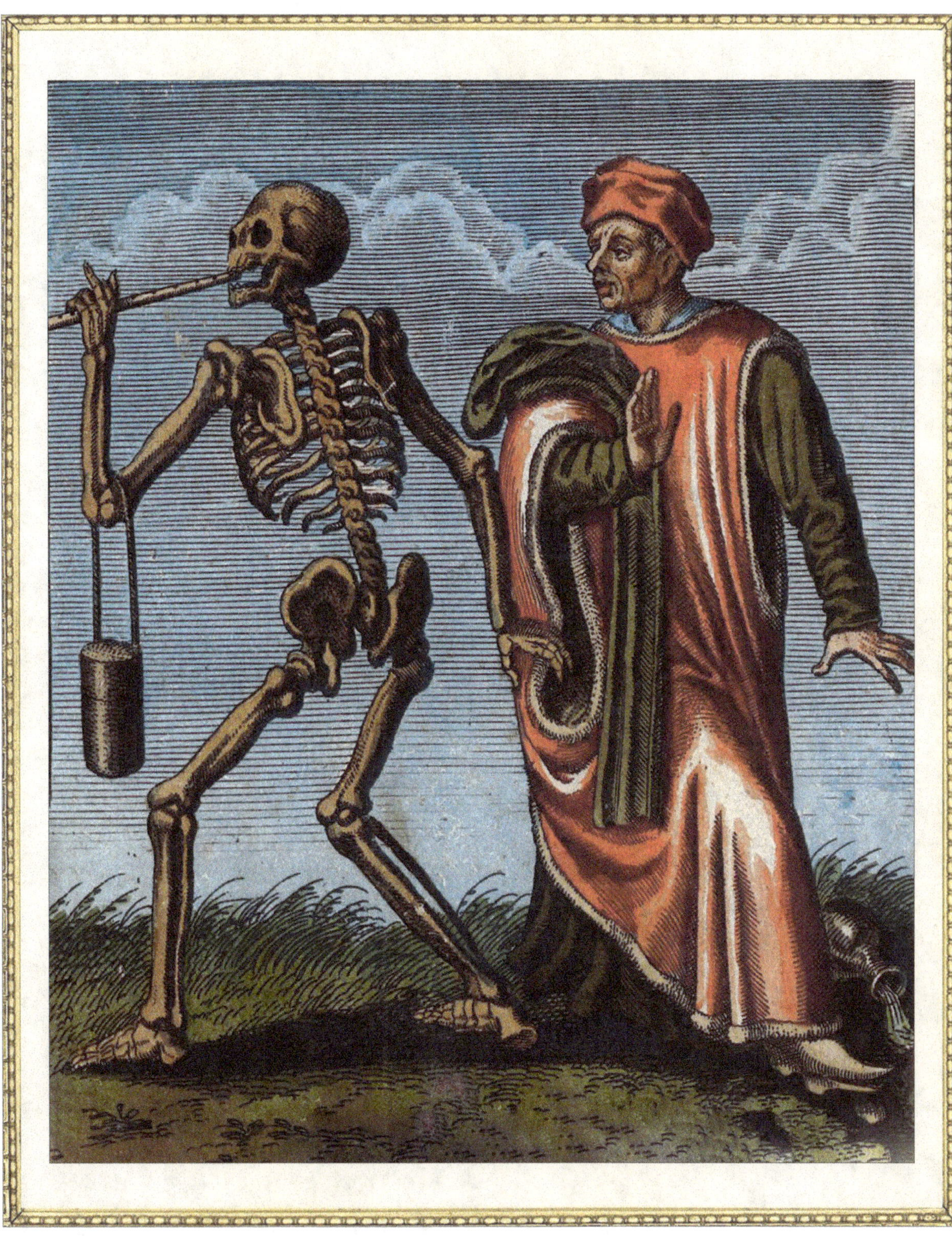

DEATH TO THE NOBLEMAN

Come hither now and play the man, you noble warrior, if you can;
if Death, who spares none, be your friend, you'll be rewarded in the end.

THE NOBLEMAN'S REPLY

Many a man I've made turn pale though cased in a coat of mail;
now comes grim death to fight with me, and brings me to extremity.

*

LA MORT AU GENTILHOMME

Revelez donc, Seigneur, ce glaive formidable,
montrez vous homme encore, et défendez vos droits...
Vain effort! Vous allez, chatelain redoutable,
recevoir sans délai le prix de vos exploits.

RÉPONSE DU GENTILHOMME

Maint brave enharnaché d'une armure pesante
succombant sous mes coups, a demandé quartier;
mais le nouveau champion qui vient me défier
terrasse sans effort ma bravoure impuissante.

*

LA MORTE AL NOBILE

Sfodera la tua spada, nobile guerriero, sii l'uomo che sei sempre stato.
Ah, è tutto invano! Pagherete immediatamente il prezzo delle vostre prodezze.

RISPOSTA DEL NOBILE

Difeso da un'armatura ho spaventato molti uomini;
ora nessun'arma mi difenderà dalla Morte, che vuole combattere con me,
portandomi allo stremo delel forze.

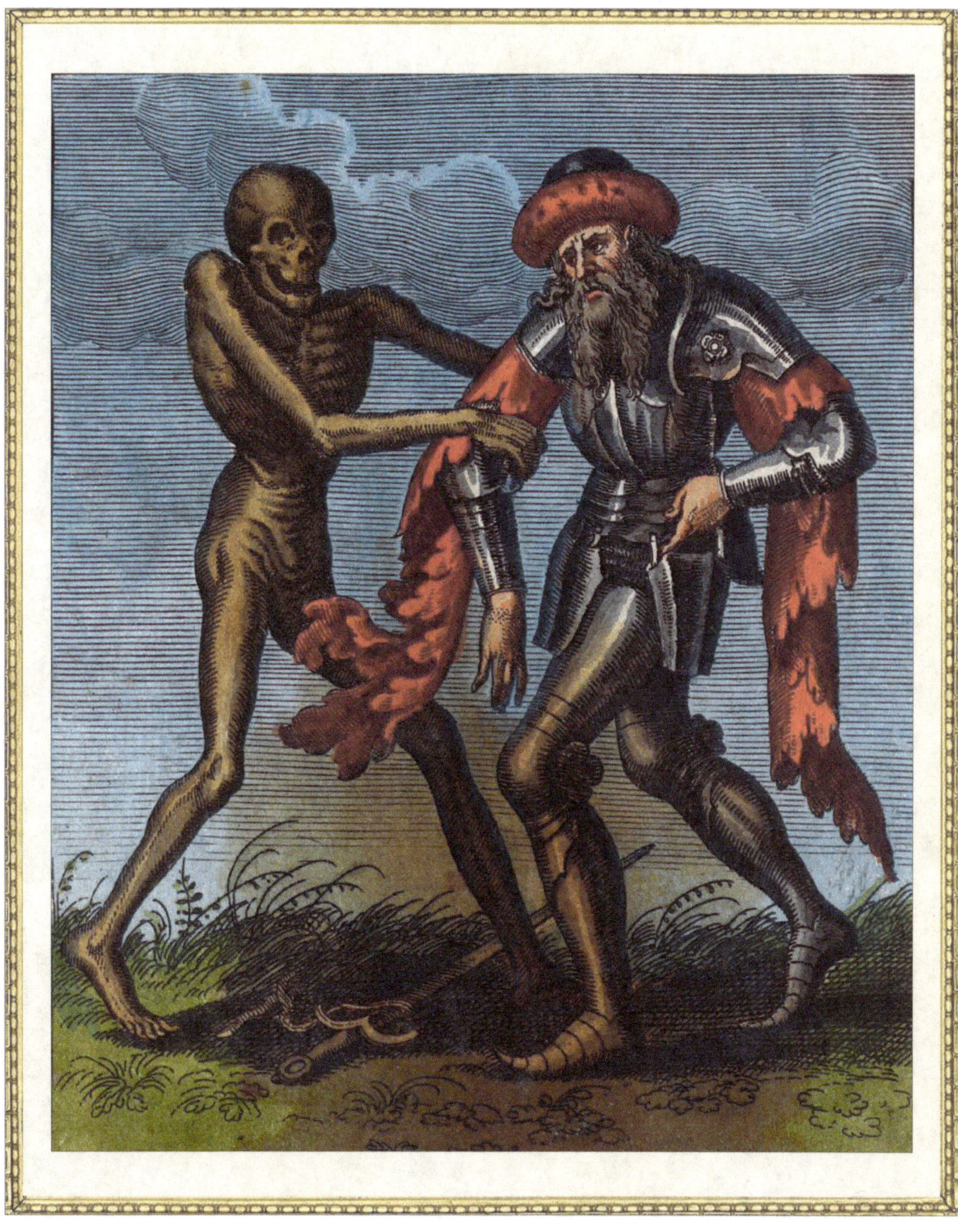

DEATH TO THE LADY
My Lady, leave your toilette's care, and for a dance with me prepare;
your golden locks can't help you here, what see you in your mirror clear?

THE LADY'S REPLY
Oh! Horror! What is this? Alas! I've seen Death's figure in my glass;
his dreadful form fills me with fright, my heart grows cold and sensless quite.

*

LA MORT A LA DAME
Eh! Que me font à moi ton rang et tes aieux,
tes traits nobles et fins, l'or de tes blonds cheveux?
Tout est fini pour toi. Regarde cette glace:
de ton minois charmant reconnais-tu la grace?

RÉPONSE DE LA DAME
O terreur! Qu'ai je vu? Découverte cruelle!
Signe horrible et certain qui me prédit mon sort!
En vain, à ce miroir autrefois si fidèle,
mes traits montrent la vie... Il réfléchit la mort!

*

LA MORTE ALLA DAMA
Salve Damigella, posso suggerirti di lasciare stare il tuo rito di bellezza?
Ora come ora i tuoi riccioli biondi non ti saranno d'aiuto...
riesci a vedermi nel tuo specchio?

RISPOSTA DELLA DAMA
Oddio! Cosa vedo? Il riflesso della Morte! Figura orribile mi attanaglia il cuore
che ormai freddo, si spegne e si addormenta.

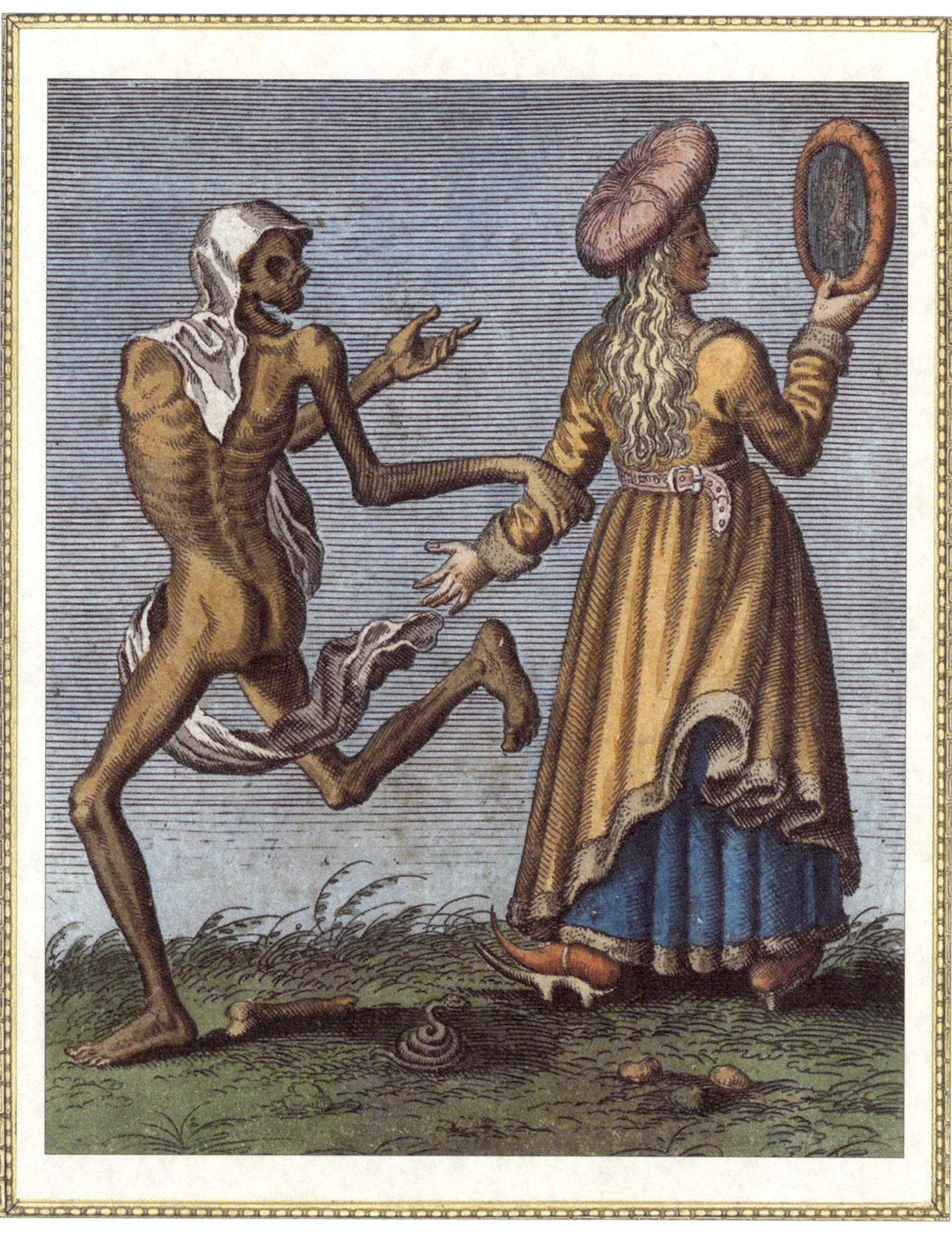

DEATH TO THE MERCHANT
Come, Merchant, let your business lie; your time is up, you now must die.
Death can't be bribed with goods or gold, so dance along, as you are told.

THE MERCHANT'S REPLY
To gather gain I've been well skilled, chests and strong boxes all are filled;
but death despises all my wealth, and robs me both of life and health.

*

LA MORT AU MARCHAND
Croyez.vous à prix d'or que vous m'engagerez
a vous vendre un seul jour, un quart d'heure de vie?
Reprenez ce métal; en vain vous me l'offrez:
vous etes le seul bien qui peut me faire envie.

RÉPONSE DU MARCHAND
Fier de mon savoir-faire, et rempli d'allégresse,
je comptais chaque jour l'or de mon coffre-fort,
et je disais: que craindre avec tant de richesse?
Mais c'est compter bien mal que compter sans la mort.

*

LA MORTE AL MERCANTE
Vieni, Mercante, fammi vedere cosa hai da offrirmi. Scherzo, la Morte non può
essere comprata da nessun bene, quindi balla con me, è un ordine!

RISPOSTA DEL MERCANTE
Ho imparato il mestiere di vendere, e l'ho fatto molto bene: ho venduto molti cestini
e ricchi scrigni. Ma la Morte rende inutile la mia fortuna, derubandomi la vita.

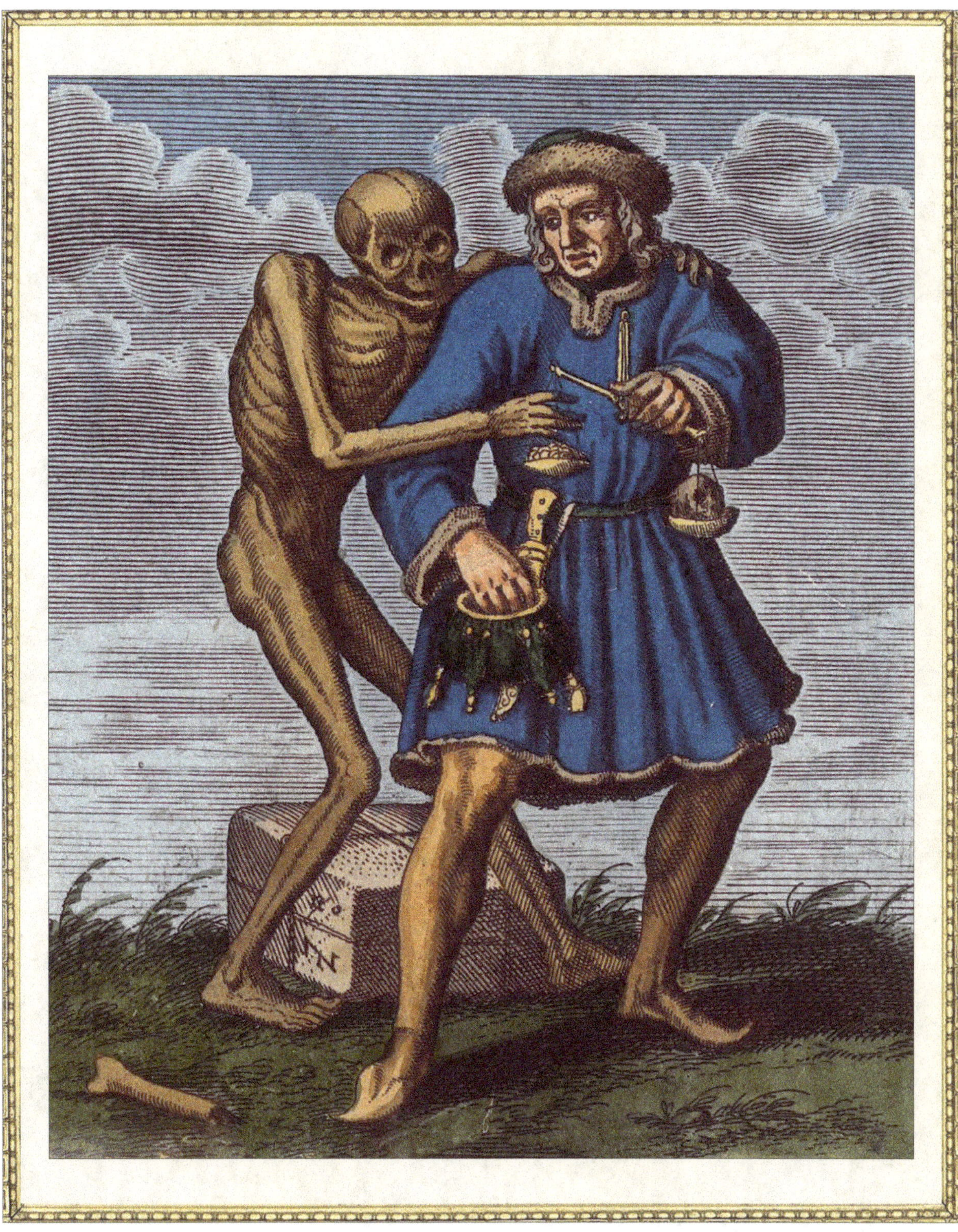

DEATH TO THE ABBESS
My lady Abbess pure and fair, how small you're grown, well, I declare!
Before I'd cast reproach on you, I'd bite my finger through and through.

THE ABBESS' REPLY
I've read my lessons from the Psalter, both in the Choir and near the altar;
but now for prayer I've no more breath, for I must go along with death.

*

LA MORT A L'ABBESSE
Dites nous, Dame Abbesse, honneur du monastère,
d'ou vient cet embonpoint qui semble vous gener?
Je ne veux rien imaginer:
mais enfin pour jamais je vais vous en défaire.

RÉPONSE DE L'ABBESSE
Au pied du saint autel, dans en pieux accord,
les vierges du seigneur et moi-meme à leur tete,
nous chantions tous les jours les hymnes du Prophete.
Oh, si ces chants divins pouvaient fléchir la mort!

*

LA MORTE ALLA BADESSA
Signora Badessa, l'orgoglio del monastero!
Hai messo su qualche chilo ultimamente?
Nessun problema, mi sbarazzerò anche di quello!

RISPOSTA DELLA BADESSA
Ai piedi dell'altare, insieme alle altre vergini del Signore, io stessa ho cantato i sacri
inni del Profeta. Oh, se questi canti potessero risparmiarmi la vita!

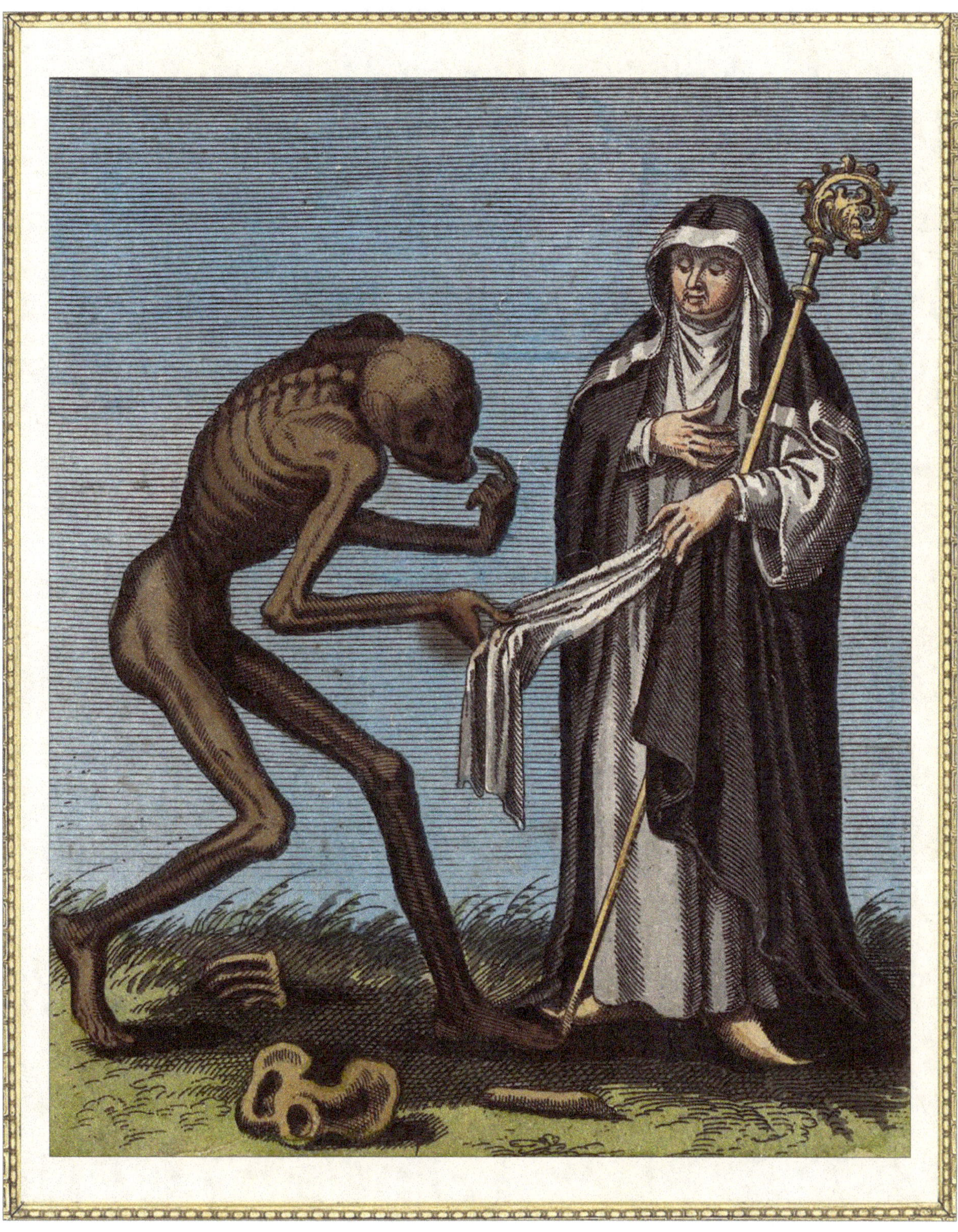

DEATH TO THE CRIPPLE
Limp this way now with thy old crutch, death will relieve thee very much;
unworthy of the world thou art, so come and in my dance take part.

THE CRIPPLE'S REPLY
A poor and lame man here on earth is for no man a friend of worth;
but death will prove his friend one day, and take him with the rich way.

*

LA MORT AU PAUVRE BOITEUX
Pauvre, vieux, impotent, que fais-tu dans le monde?
Un mortel comme toi n'est pour lui qu'un fardeau;
mais pour moi, tout est bon; le pauvre dans ma ronde
danse l'égal des rois: c'est la loi du tombeau.

RÉPONSE DU PAUVRE BOITEUX
Dans ce monde, insensible au sort de l'indigence,
le pauvre estropié n'a jamais eu d'amis;
la mort seule veut l'etre; et, grace à sa puissance,
dans les rangs des humains je bais me voir admis.

*

LA MORTE ALLO STORPIO
Cosa ci fa ancora al mondo un povero, vecchio, storpio come te?
Agli occhi del mondo non sei nessuno, ma non ti preoccupare: per la legge
dell'oltretombe sei tale quale un re.

RISPOSTA DELLO STORPIO
Qui sulla terra un vecchio impotente come me non ha amici, e non è amico di
nessuno. Forse almeno la morte mi accetterà fra i suoi, in compagnia di ricchi e
nobili.

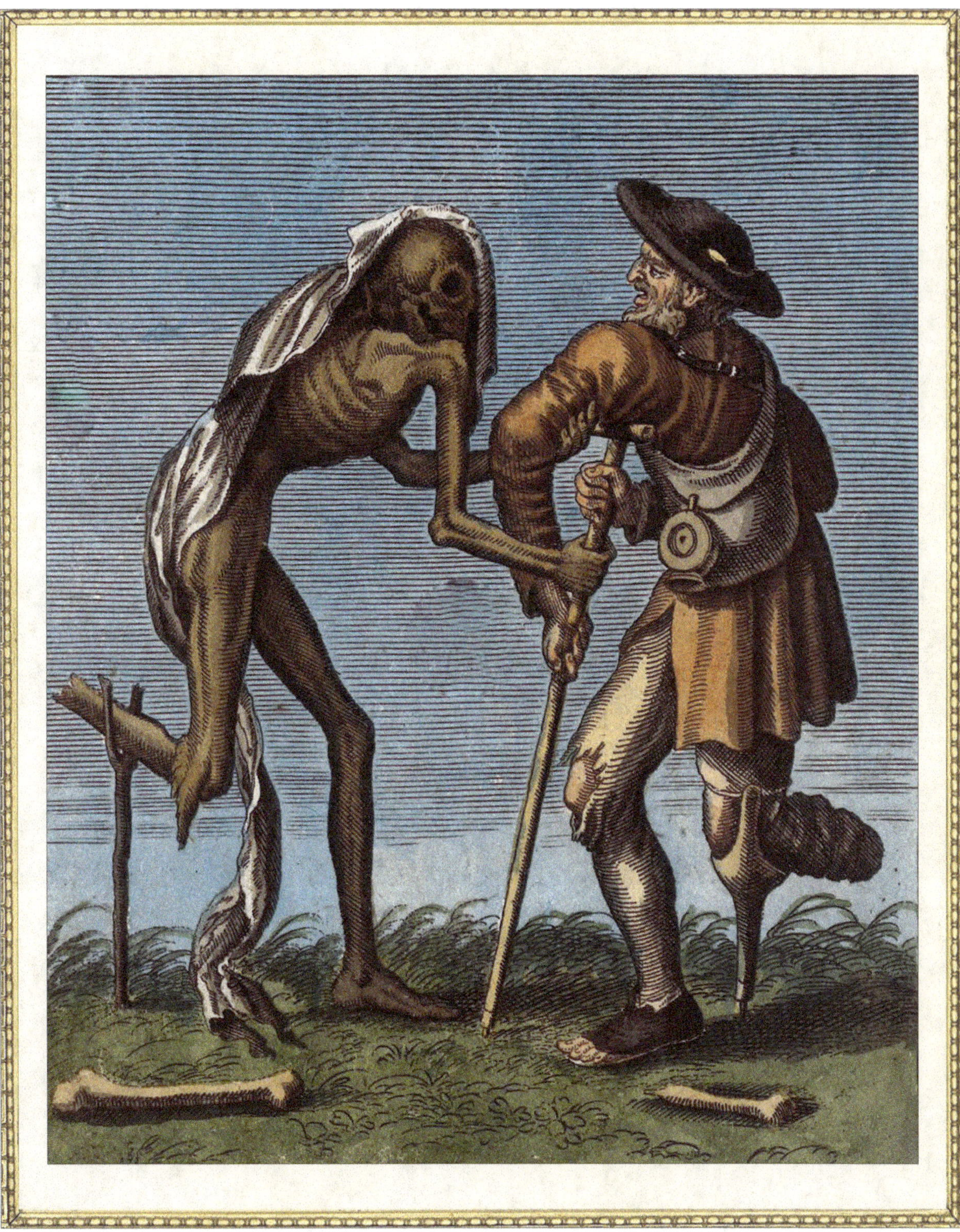

DEATH TO THE HERMIT
Come, Brother, from thy cell away, stand still; thy light I quench for aye,
for thous must trudge with me tonight, with thy old beard so long and white.

THE HERMIT'S REPLY
For a long time I've worn through vow a hairy shirt; 'tis useless now,
'gainst death my cell is no defence. My prayer time's up: I must go hence.

*

LA MORT A L'ERMITE
Bon ermite, si tard, loin de votre chapelle,
une lanterne en main, où portez-vous vos pas?
Vous n'irez pas bien loin; j'éteins votre chandelle,
et m'en vais vous conduire où vous ne pensez pas.

RÉPONSE DE L'ERMITE
Ma cellule, disais-je, obscure et solitaire;
est sure. Vain espoir! Où n'entre pas la mort?
Et que me sert encore d'avoir porté la haire?
Pourrai-je avec ma haire apaiser le Dieu fort?

*

LA MORTE ALL'EREMITA
Buon eremita, dove vai così tardi e con quella lanterna in mano? Non andrete
lontano, questo è certo. Ora spegnerò la tua lanterna e vi condurrò dove non osate
neanche immaginare.

RISPOSTA DELL'EREMITA
Pensavo che la mia tana, oscura e solitaria, fosse sicura, ma mi sbagliavo. Dove non
può entrare la morte? E a che mi serve ora la mia barba? Farò forse più felice Dio
con la mia barba?

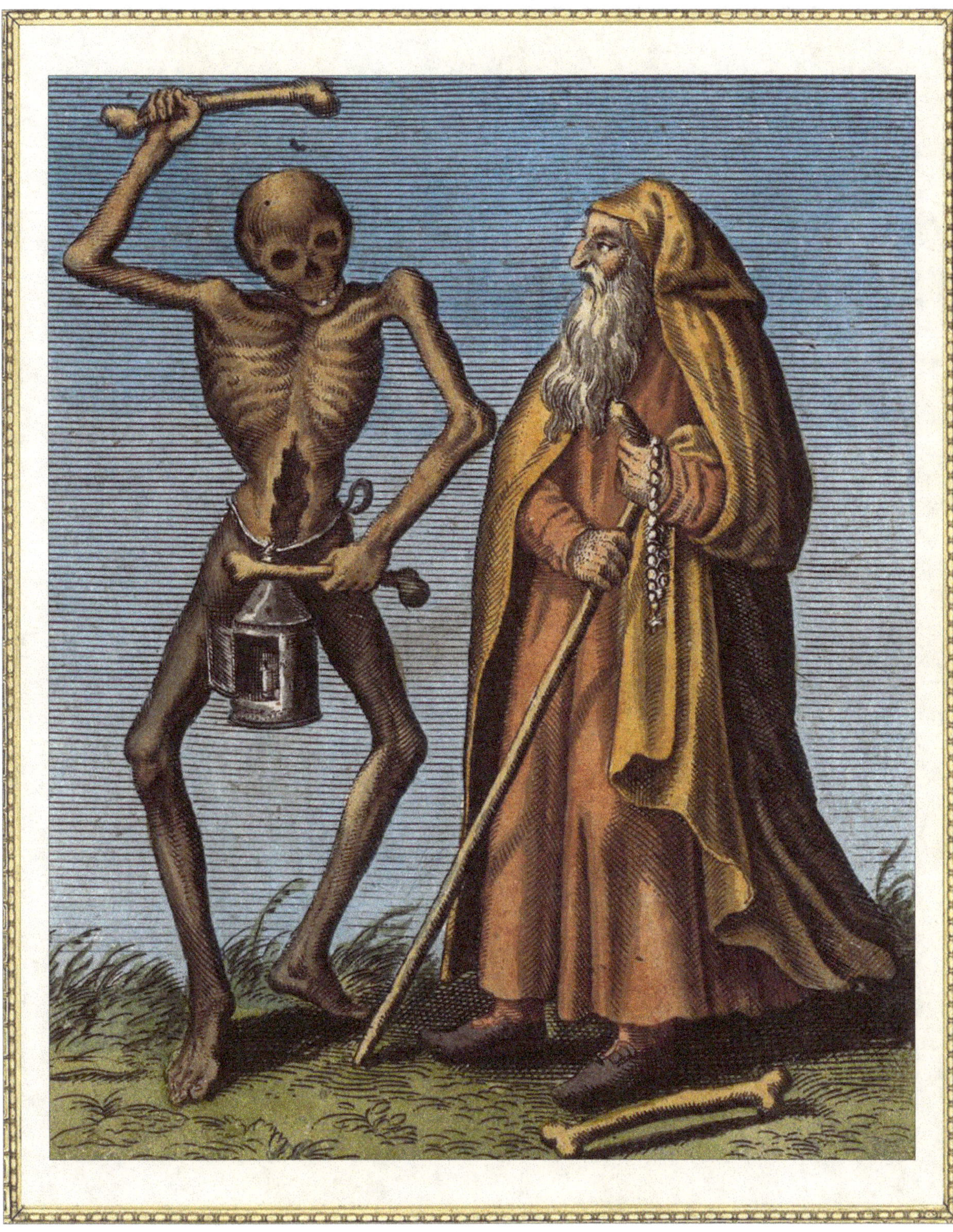

DEATH TO THE YOUNG MAN

Tell me, o Youth, where wilt thou go? A way you think not of I'll shew;
where all thy comrades choice are found. Such is my message, short and round.

THE YOUNG MAN'S REPLY

In riot, lust and banquets sweet, and nightly woings in the street,
my youth I sought in mirth to spend, and little thought it thus would end.

*

LA MORT AU JEUNE HOMME

Holà, jeune homme, arrete; où vas-tu de ce pas?
Rire, chanter, danser, et courtiser les femmes?
Laisse aux vivants le soin de divertir les dames,
et dans un autre lieu viens prendre tes ébats.

RÉPONSE DU JEUNE HOMME

Grand rieur, grand buveur, et cher aux demoiselles,
j'ai de tous les plaisirs pris une doble part;
mais parmi les festins et les faveurs des belles,
qui va songer, hélas, à l'heure du départ?

*

LA MORTE AL GIOVANOTTO

Dove stai andando, ragazzo? Certo, a ridere, cantare, e corteggiare le belle ragazze.
Lascia ai vivi tali piaceri, e vieni a ballare con me da un'altra parte.

RISPOSTA DEL GIOVANOTTO

Ho passato la mia giovinezza nel caos, tra preziosi banchetti e divertimenti sfrenati,
mai pensando che un giorno potessero finire.

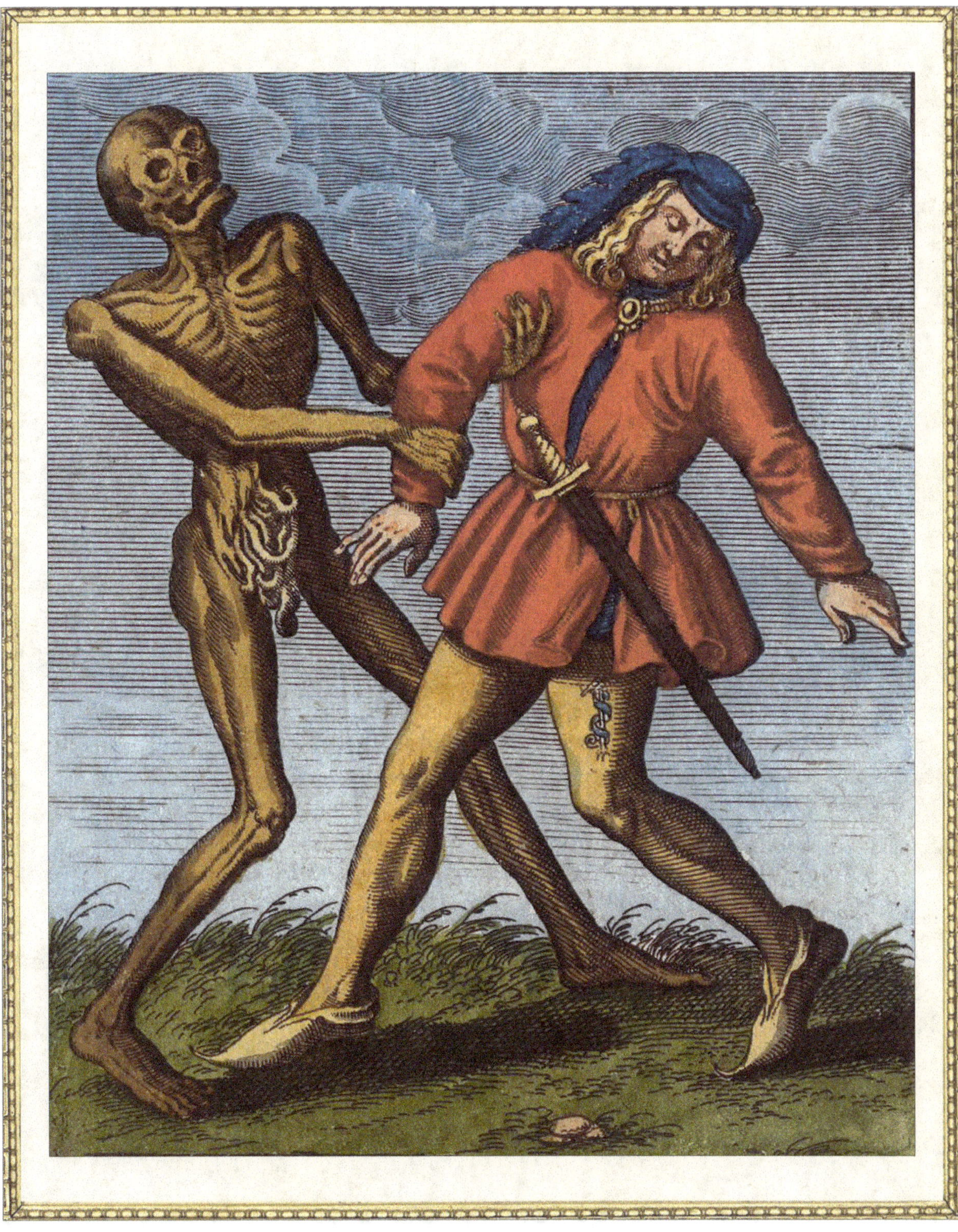

DEATH TO THE USURER

Not to thy gold my hand I stretch, thou Usurer, ungodly wretch;
from Christ thou didst not learn thy trade, therefore black death thy guide is made.

THE USURER'S REPLY

By Christ's commands, I set no store; my usury produced me more.
Now all in others hands remains, useless my scraping toil and gains.

*

LA MORT A L'USURIER

Infame usurier, ame vile,
est-ce ainsi que tu suis la loi de l'Évangile?
Reprends, reprends ton or, et de ce pas, voleur,
suis les traces d'un guide aussi noir que ton coeur.

RÉPONSE DE L'USURIER

Je me souciais peu de cette loi sévère;
je disais: mon métier produit plus et vaut mieux;
et maintenant il faut laisser tout sur la terre...
Que me sert désormais ce commerce odieux?

*

LA MORTE ALL'USURAIO

Infame e vile usuraio, credi di essere la legge del Vangelo?
Tieniti il tuo oro, non m'interessa, vieni piuttosto con una guida più nera
del tuo stesso cuore.

RISPOSTA DELL'USURAIO

Mi sono preoccupato poco del giudizio divino; mi dicevo "Più produco, meglio è".
Adesso che devo lasciare tutto su questa terra, a cosa mi è servito questo odioso
lavoro?

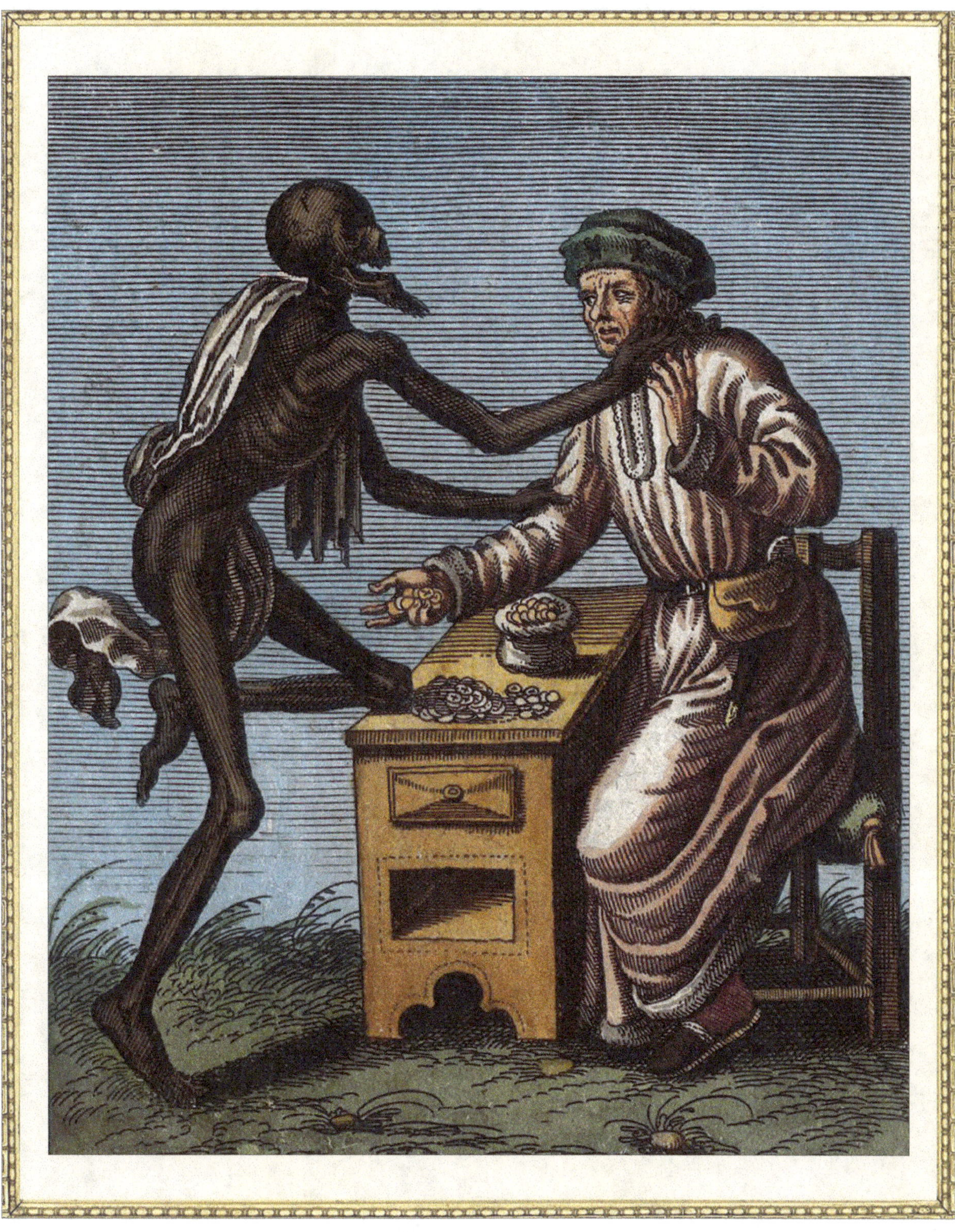

DEATH TO THE MAIDEN

Maiden! Your lips so fresh and red must with paleness overspread;
you've danced with boys in joy and glee, now comes the time to dance with me.

THE MAIDEN'S REPLY

Alas! Thy dread hand holds me fast, my mirth and joy are all now past;
no more in dance I'll take delight, to all I say: a long good night.

*

LA MORT A LA JEUNE FILLE

La paleur se répand sur votre beau visage;
jeune fille, il est temps: disposez votre coeur;
on briguait votre main aux bals du voisinage
vous n'aurez désormais que moi seul pour danseur.

RÉPONSE DE LA JEUNE FILLE

Monstre horrible, ta main glacée
fait passer le frisson jusqu'au fond de mon coeur.
Quoi! Mon bonheur a fui! Quoi! Ma vie est passée!
O souvenirs amers! O regrets! O douleur!

*

LA MORTE ALLA FANCIULLA

Il pallore risplende sul tuo viso, bellissima fanciulla, ma è tempo di andare.
Dopo aver ballato con tanti giovani ora avrai solo me come compagno di danza.

RISPOSTA DELLA FANCIULLA

Mostro orribile, la tua mano è così ghiacciata che mi si è gelato il cuore.
Ah! La mia gioia è finita! Oh, amari ricordi! Oh, dolore!

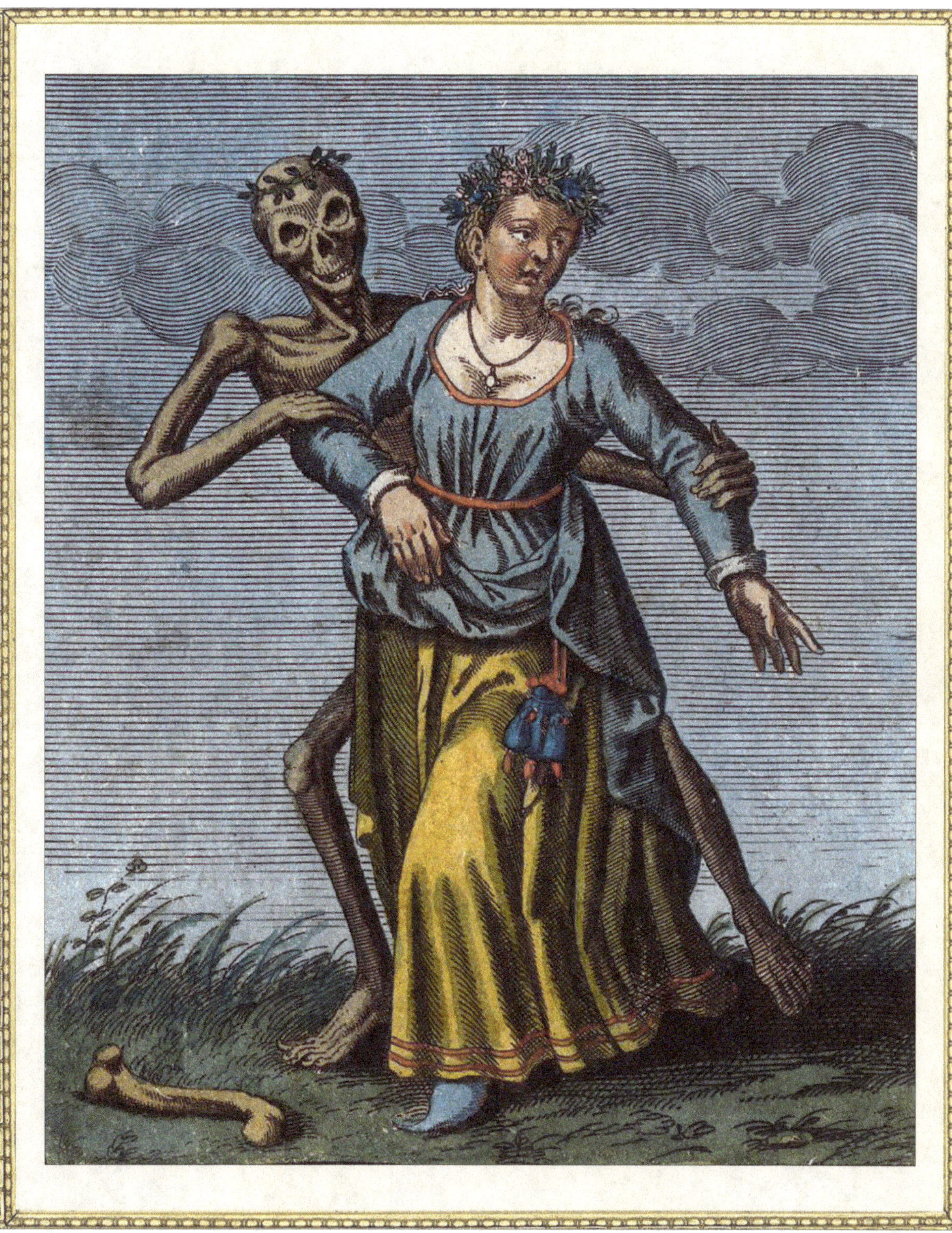

DEATH TO THE MINSTREL

What reel or jig shall we now play? The beggar? Or the Black boy?
Say, my Minstrel, for were you not there, imperfect were both dance and air.

THE MINSTREL'S REPLY

No market was to far from me, in all I gained my penny fee;
but now 'tis done and go I must, my pipe is fallen in the dust.

*

LA MORT AU MÉNÉTRIER

Ca, quel air allons nous jouer?
Quoi? La chanson du Gueux, ou l'air du Pot qui danse?
Mais le jeu ne vaut rien, il le faut avouer,
si tu n'y viens sauter pour marquer la cadence.

RÉPONSE DU MÉNÉTRIER

Il n'étoit point de fete où, malgré la distance,
on ne me vit porter mon instrument joyeux;
adieu tous mes profits! Sa bruyante cadence
ne doit plus animer les danses ni les jeux.

*

LA MORTE AL MENESTRELLO

Forza Menestrello mio, cosa cantiamo ora? Una supplica? O cos'altro?
Ammettilo, insieme formiamo una bella coppia di suonatori imperfetti.

RISPOSTA DEL MENESTRELLO

In ogni luogo dove sono stato, non importa quanto lontano stesse, mi hanno dato
qualche moneta. Ora è tutto finito, e il mio flauto è caduto nell'abisso con me.

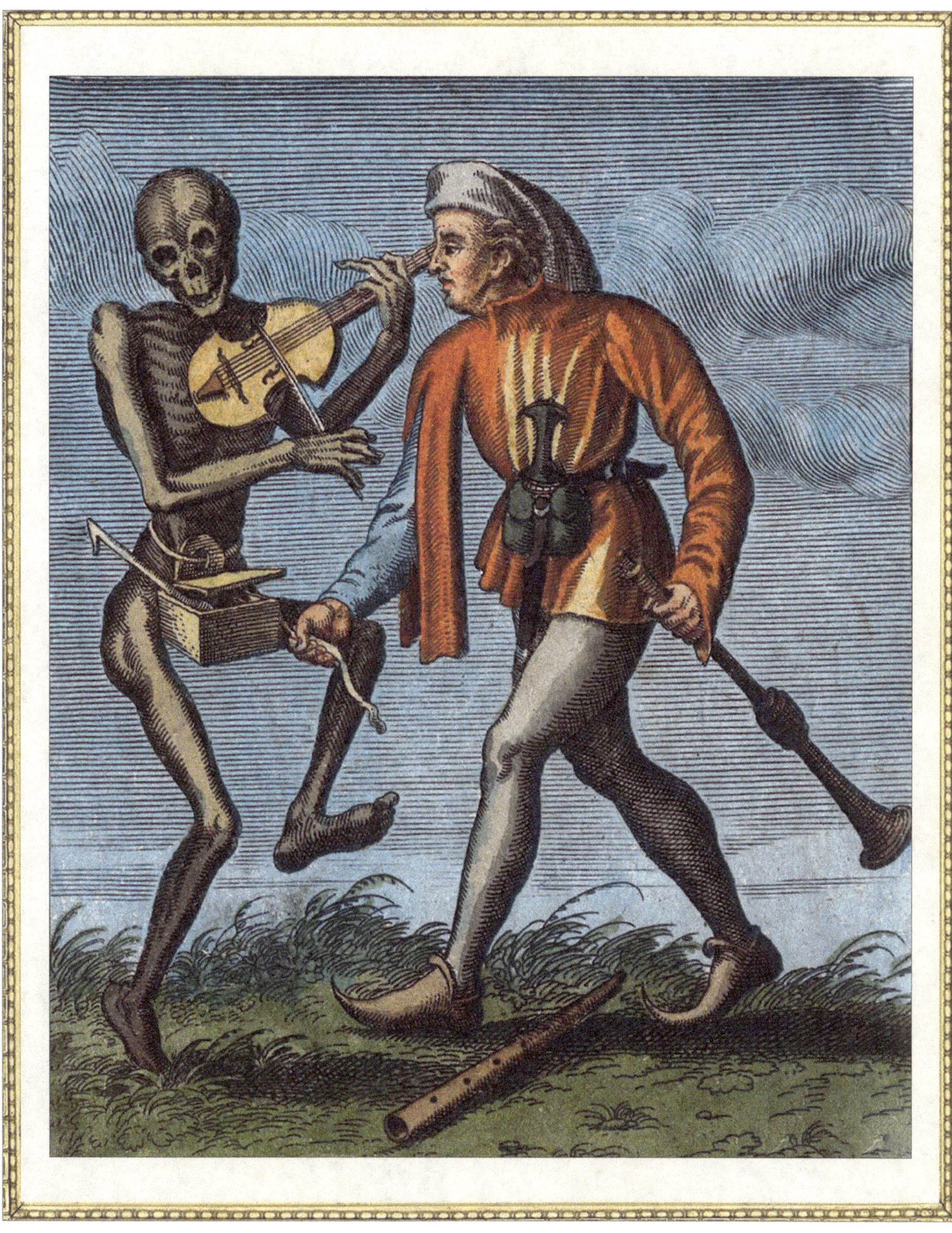

DEATH TO THE HERALD
Herald! In thy red cap so grand, on thee I now must lay my hand;
to princes you were ever dear, now cast your gilded staff down here.

THE HERALD'S REPLY
The Emeperor's favourite was I, my horse and purse he did supply:
my voice has oft made many quiver, now death has stopped my mouth for ever.

*

LA MORT AU HÉRAUT
Ton chaperon de pourpre et ta faveur passée
ne te sauveront pas; et ce sceptre emprunté,
symbole du pouvoir d'un maitre redouté,
va tomber de ta main glacée.

RÉPONSE DU HÉRAUT
Aimé du souverain, j'ai souvent en son nom
a de fiers ennemis annoncé sa vengeance;
mais la mort, sans respect pour mon puissant patron,
a réduit à néant toute mon éloquence.

*

LA MORTE ALL'ARALDO
Il tuo cappello vermiglio e la tua fedeltà non ri salveranno; e quello scettro preso in prestito al tuo temuto padrone cadrà all'istante dalla tua mano ghiacciata.

RISPOSTA DELL'ARALDO
Ero il preferito del sovrano, e a molte fiere ho annunciato il suo nome. Ma la morte non ha rispetto del mio padrone e rende nulla la mia eloquenza.

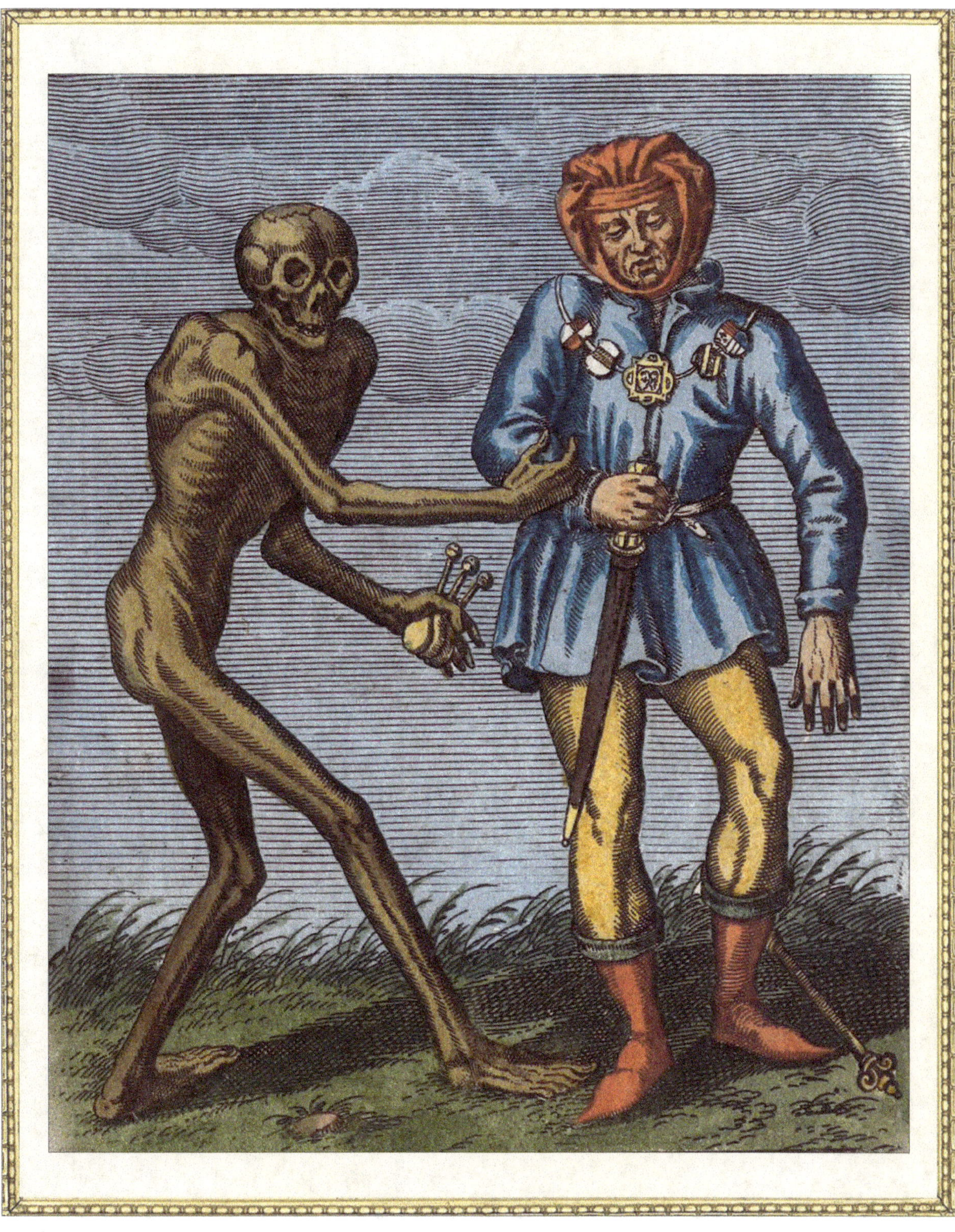

DEATH TO THE MAYOR
'Tis time, o Mayor, to lay to heart, that soul and body once must part;
while on my lyre this truth I sing, take heed, and to my music spring.

THE MAYOR'S REPLY
With care I've done my duty long, and hope that none has suffered wrong;
when rich and poor shall judged be, o God! Have mercy upon me!

*

LA MORT AU MAIRE
Maire, voici linstant où l'ame délivrée
brise des fers honteux et sort de sa prison:
de ma lyre funèbre entends le grave son
t'annoncer l'heure désirée.

RÉPONSE DU MAIRE
J'ai chéri mes devoirs, et, d'une main loyale
j'ai taché de tenir une balance égale
entre le riche et l'indigent:
puisse pour mes erreurs mon juge etre indulgent!

*

LA MORTE AL SINDACO
Sindaco, è arrivata l'ora per la tua anima di uscire dalla prigione: senti la mia lira
funebre...sta annunciando la tua ora.

RISPOSTA DEL SINDACO
Ho amato i miei doveri, e ho sempre cercato di essere impari con i ricchi e con i
poveri. Per questo possa il giudice dell'aldilà essere indulgente con me!

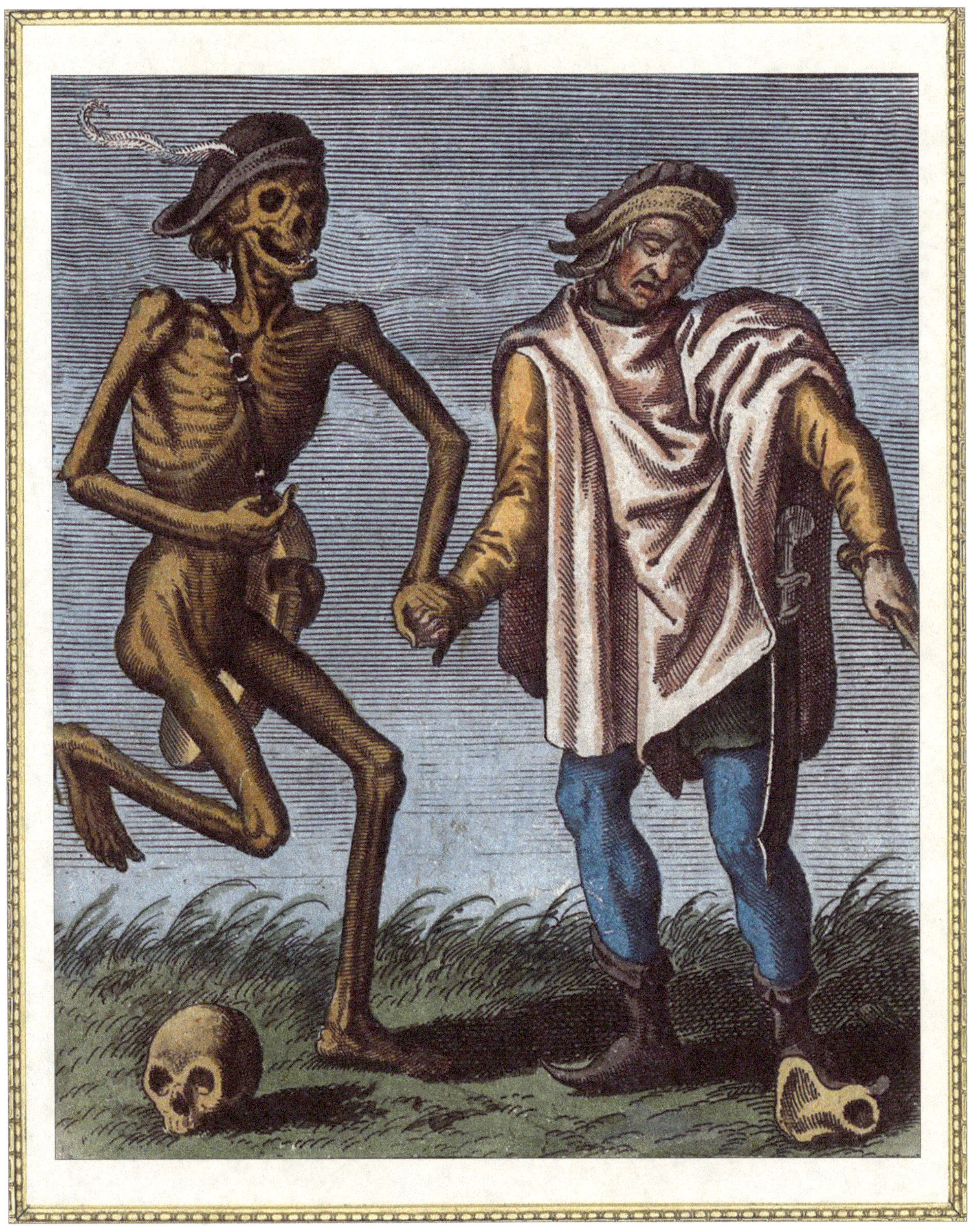

DEATH TO THE HEADSMAN

Are you the sharp dread man of law? Whose coat and cap keep rogues in awe;
your look is sour, but what care I, to change my sentence none need try.

THE HEADSMAN'S REPLY

No one by me was e'er oppress'd I but fulfilled the law's behest,
from all the same respect I claimed and King's head-minister was named.

*

LA MORT AU GRAND PRÉVOT

Seigneur au manteau rouge, autre fois soudoyé
pour remplir ici-bas un sanglant ministère,
tes larmes ne me touchent guère;
tu viendras où ton glaive en a tant envoyé.

RÉPONSE DU GRAND PRÉVOT

Devant ton tribunal, juge saint et sévère,
le sang que j'ai versé ne m'accusera pas;
j'ai servi de nos lois la rigueur salutaire;
l'ennemi seul des lois a redouté mon bras.

*

LA MORTE AL BOIA

Tu, signore dagli indumenti rossi ed aspri, hai vissuto per compiere un sanguinario
mestiere, quindi le tue lacrime non mi toccheranno: verrai nel luogo dove hai
mandato tu stesso molta gente.

RISPOSTA DEL BOIA

Davanti al tuo tribunale, giudice santo e severo, il sangue che ho versato non può
essere un'accusa. Ho rispettato gli ordini datomi e solo i nemici della patria hanno
provato la mia spada!

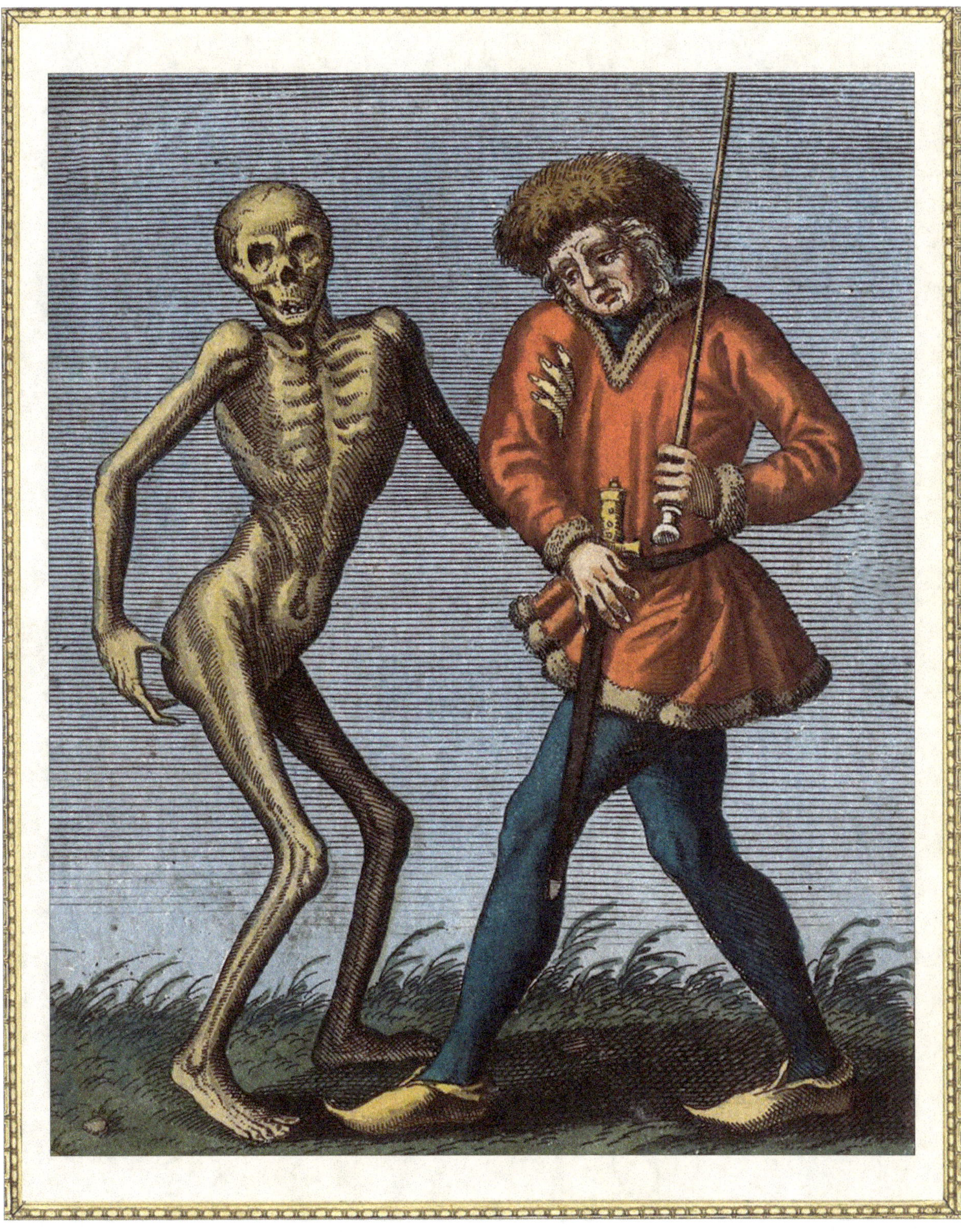

DEATH TO THE JESTER
Come Hal, dance now without a jest, gird up loins and do your best;
your club you may leave on the ground, my dance will sweat you, i'll be bound.

THE JESTER'S REPLY
Woe's me! I'd carry wood or clay, and blows endure four times a day;
from Master and from servants all, rather then hear this dry man's call.

*

LA MORT AU BOUFFON
Tu te plais à sauter: eh bien! saute, Bouffon;
mon jeu ferait suer le fou le plus agile
mais laisse pour toujours ta marotte inutile:
tes farces parmi nous ne sont plus de saison.

RÉPONSE DU BOUFFON
Oh! Que j'aimerais mieux n'etre qu'un pauvre diable,
porter de lourds fardeaux, etre chargé de coups,
que de suivre ce monstre à face epouvantable,
qui ne respecte rien, non pas meme les fous!

*

LA MORTE AL GIULLARE
E così ti piace saltare, eh giullare? Ebbene salta! Suderai molto, ma saranno gli
ultimi salti che farai...ti conviene farli molto bene.

RISPOSTA DEL GIULLARE
Preferirei essere un povero diavolo, uno schiavo, fare lavori pesanti piuttosto che
essere portato via da questo mucchio d'ossa che non ha rispetto per nessuno, men
che meno per i matti come me.

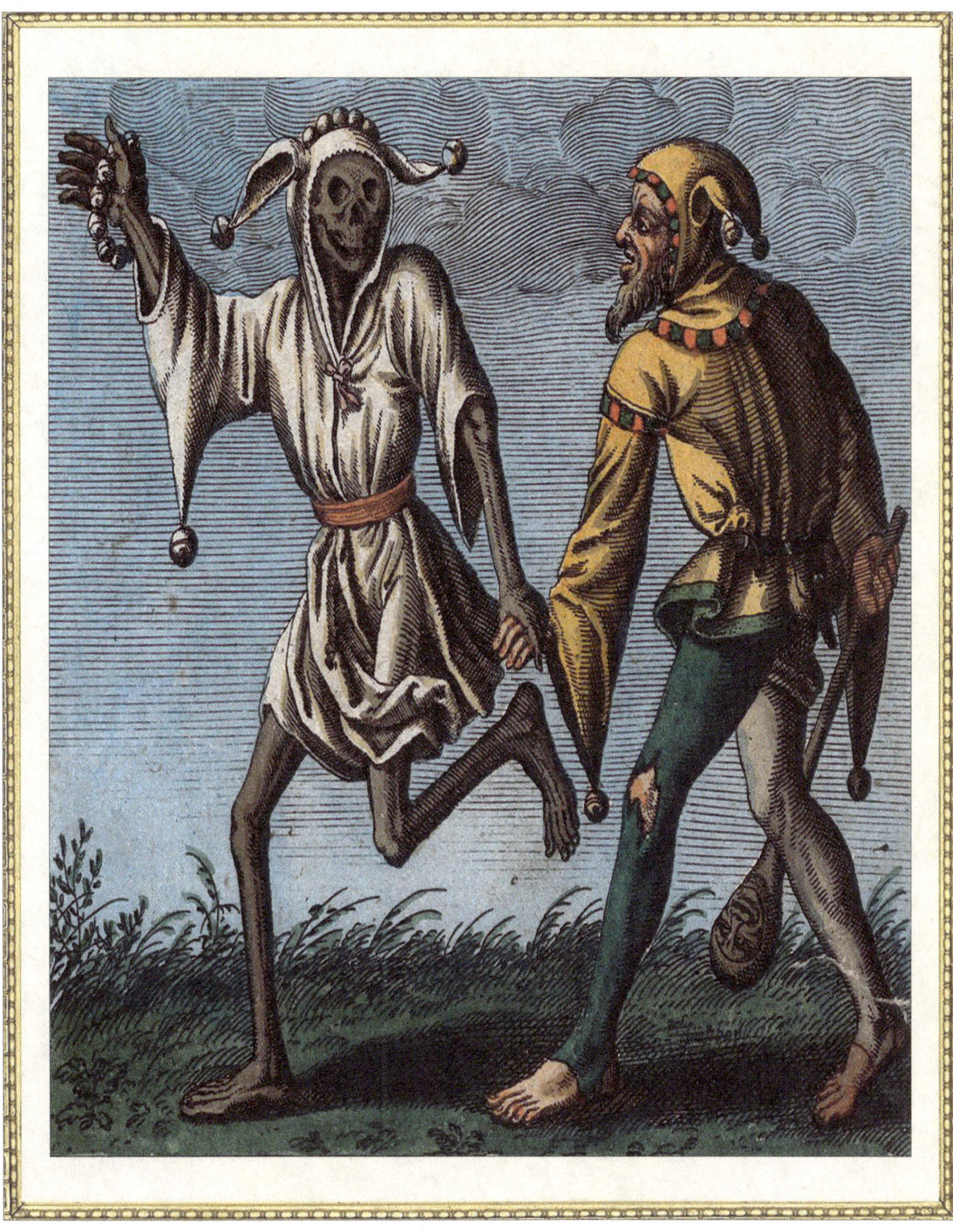

DEATH TO THE PEDLAR

Come hither, Pedlar, Penny snatch, you common cheat and noisy wretch;
now follow me, some other blade will gladly carry on your trade.

THE PEDLAR'S REPLY

Throughout the world I long have ranged and money of all sorts exchanged,
pounds, dollars, crowns and farthings too; o Death, who'll pay me now what's due?

*

LA MORT AU MERCIER

Depuis assez longtemps, docteur en tricherie,
avec tès riens brillants tu cours per le pays;
laisse à ton concurrent qui meurt de jalousie
ton industrie et tes profits.

RÉPONSE DU MERCIER

O combien cette mercerie
dans mes habiles mains aurait fructifié!
O mort! Attends du moins, attends, je t'en supplie,
que mes débiteurs m'aient payé!

*

LA MORTE AL VENDITORE AMBULANTE

Vieni qui, ladruncolo imbroglione e, se posso permettermi, anche fastidioso.
Seguimi e qualche altro farabutto porterà avanti il tuo commercio.

RISPOSTA DEL VENDITORE AMBULANTE

Ho viaggiato in tutto il mondo e scambiato qualsiasi soldo; scudi, corone e anche
semplici quattrini. O morte, chi mi farà pagare ora il conto di tutto ciò?

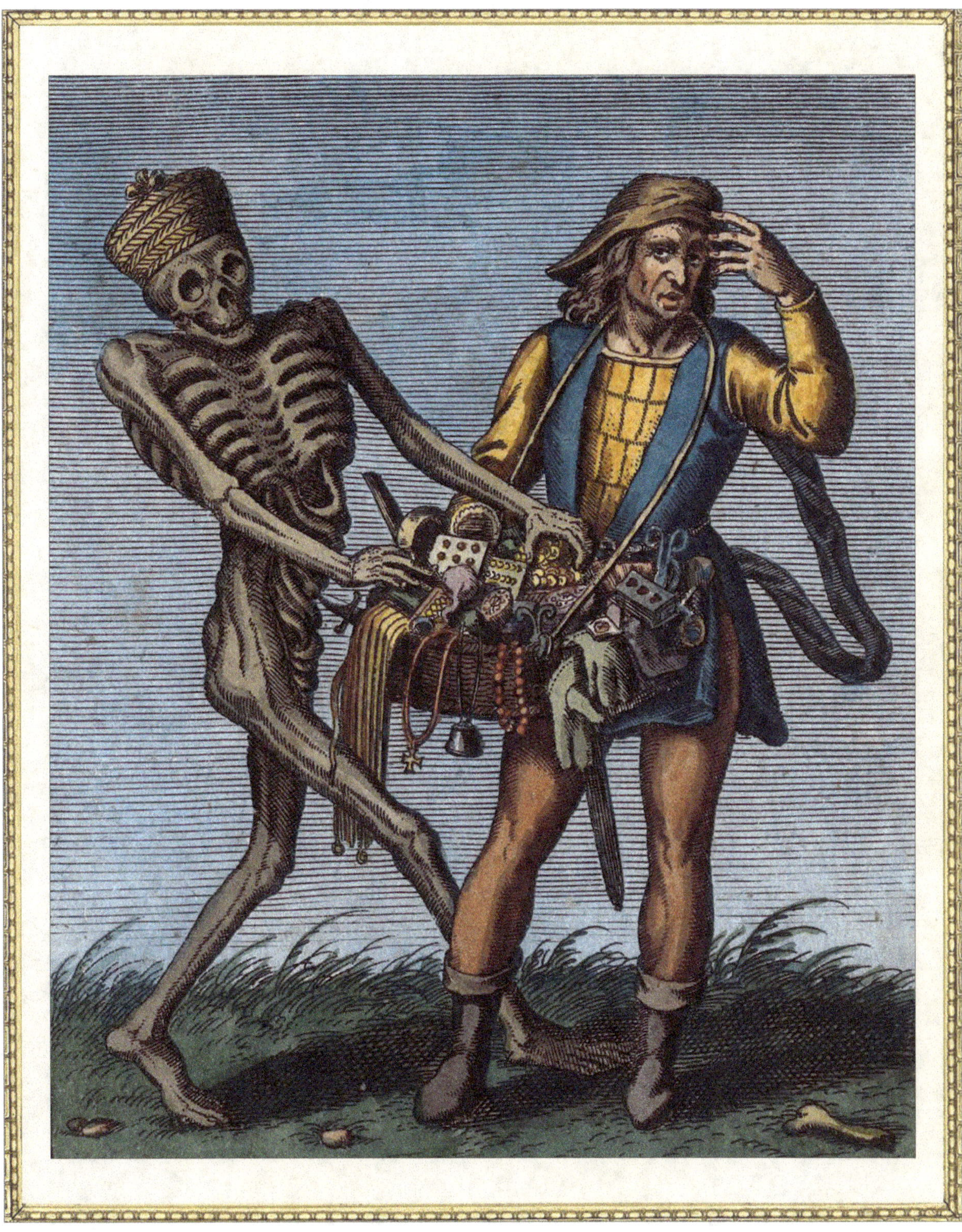

DEATH TO THE BLIND MAN
Here I cut off your leader small, hold short, else in the ditch you'll fall;
you poor, lind, old and useless one with your worn coat, torn, patched & done.

THE BLIND MAN'S REPLY
A poor blind man I must be led and cannot earn my daily bread:
without my dog I'm stuck quite fast, thank God my hour has come at last.

*

LA MORT A L'AVEUGLE
Pauvre aveugle en haillons, d'un coup de mes ciseaux,
je vais te priver de ton guide;
prends garde maintenant, prends bien garde, invalide;
la mort devant tes pas a tendu ses panneaux.

RÉPONSE DE L'AVEUGLE
Plaignez l'homme qui perd la vue:
sans ami, sans gite et sans bien,
qu'on lui prenne son pauvre chien,
la mort sera la bien venue.

*

LA MORTE AL CIECO
Ecco qui, cosa succede se taglio il guinzaglio della tua guida? Cadrai, povero vecchio
inutile cieco, chiuso nel tuo cappotto strappato e malconcio.

RISPOSTA DEL CIECO
Senza la mia guida non potrò guadagnare il mio pane quotidiano.
L'hai detto, sono un povero vecchio cieco, e senza cane non sopravviverò.
Grazie a Dio è giunta la mia ora.

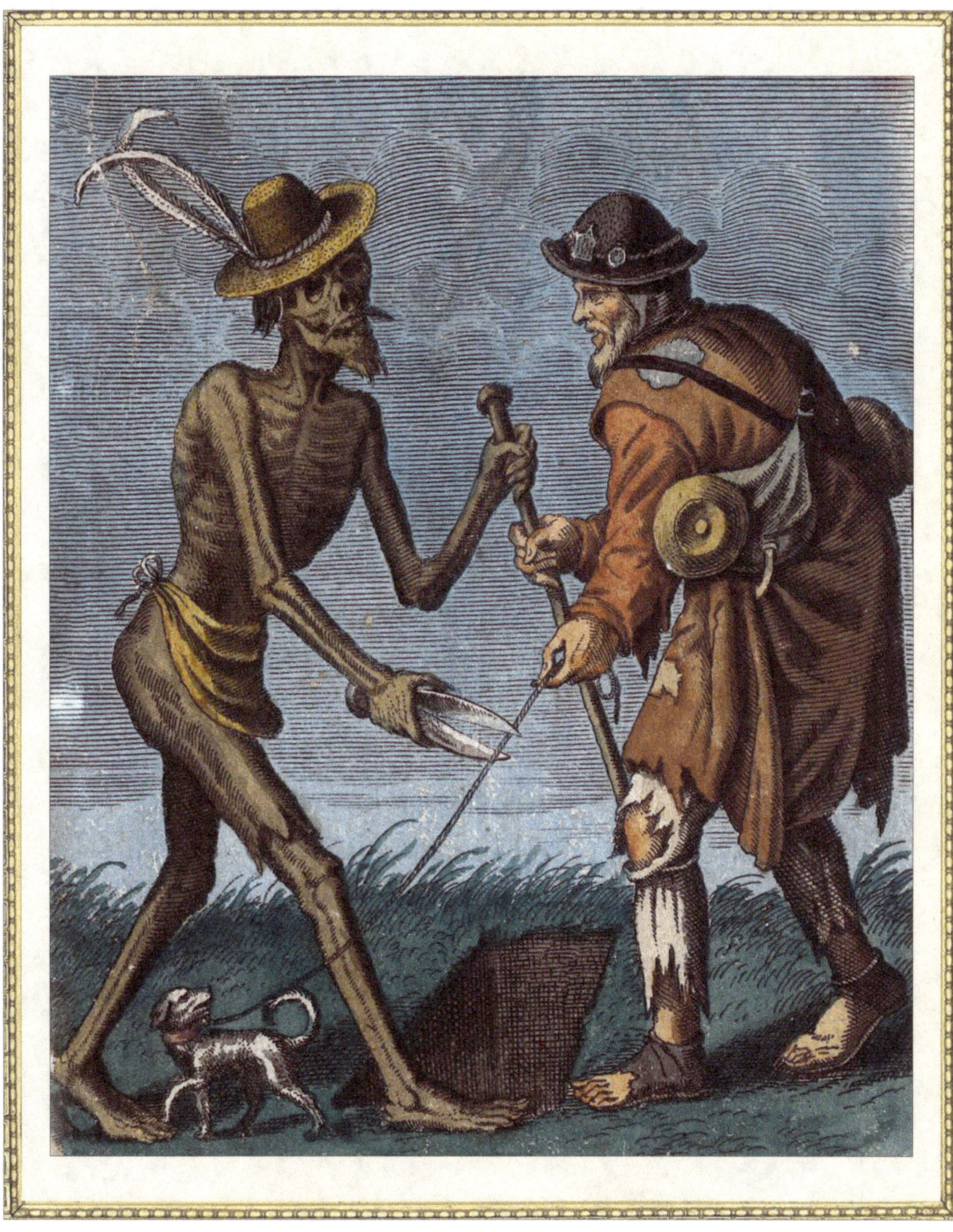

DEATH TO THE JEW
Up, Jew, and take the common gate, in vain you for Messiah wait;
Christ, whom, you slew, was He indeed, you've follow'd long a hopeless creed.

THE JEW'S REPLY
As Rabbi long the law I knew, but poison from its pages drew;
Messiah had few charms for me, my faith was Gold and Usury.

*

LA MORT AU JUIF
Malheureux juif, hate-toi de me suivre!
Ton peuple ota du nombre des vivants
celui par qui tont homme doit revivre:
viens, ton erreur a duré trop longtemps.

RÉPONSE DU JUIF
Maitre et docteur dans la sainte-Écriture,
dont je n'ai su pour moi tirer que du venin,
je m'occupai beaucoup d'une coupable usure,
et fort peu du sauveur promis au genre humain.

*

LA MORTE ALL'EBREO
Vieni, disgraziato Ebreo, è inutile che aspetti il Messia; infatti era Cristo, quello che
avete ucciso. Hai seguito a lungo un credo senza speranza.

RISPOSTA DELL'EBREO
Conosco le sacre leggi, ma so anche che dalle pagine di quel libro sgorga tanto
veleno. Non ho creduto tanto al Messia, la mia fede erano l'oro e l'usura.

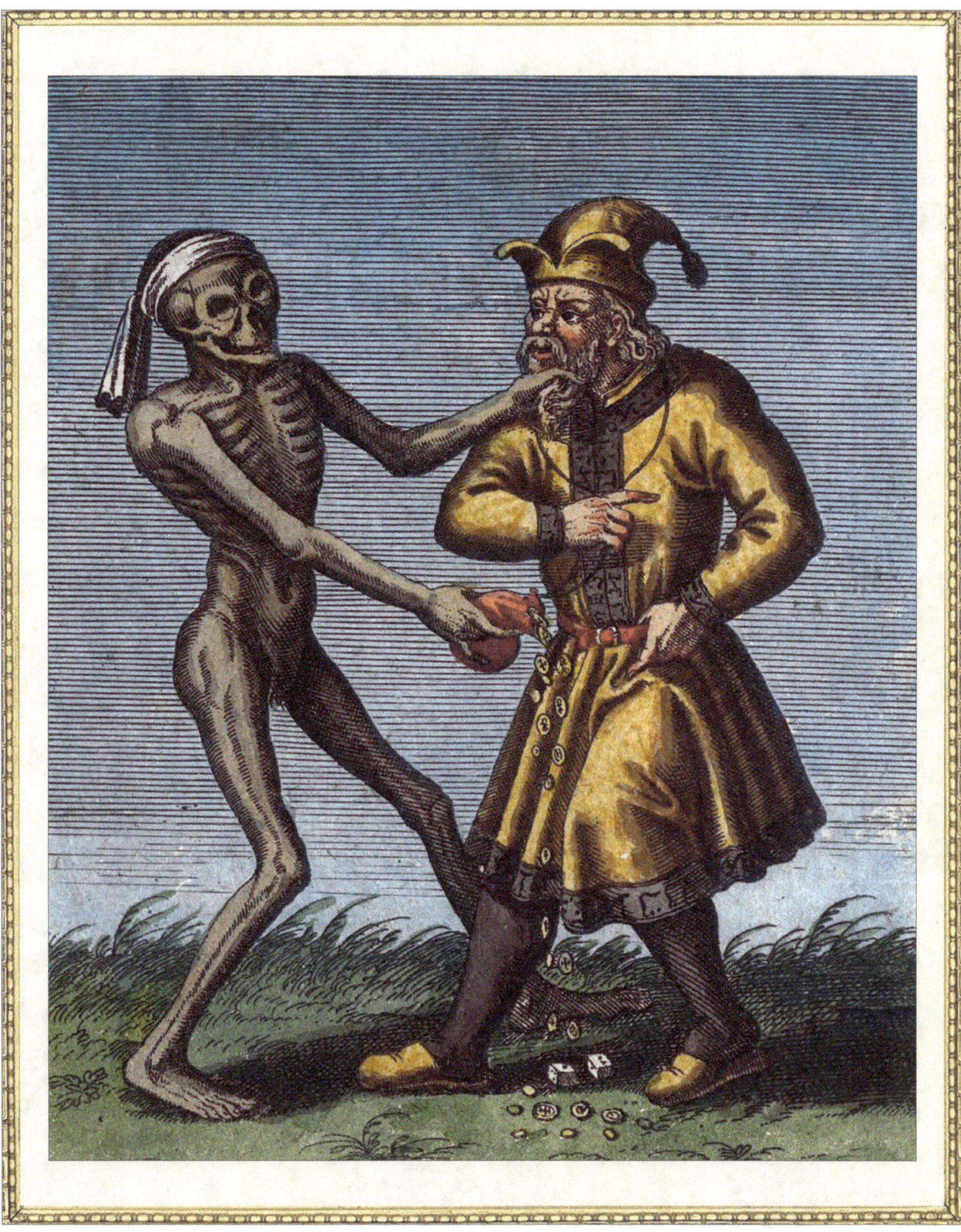

DEATH TO THE PAGAN
Come, godless man and truthless whelp, your idol now can give no help;
Satan you did as God revere, now to your prayer he gives ear.

THE PAGAN'S REPLY
Jupiter, Neptune and Pluto, ye gods supreme, don't leave me so,
if you're immortal, all you three, if not, Saturn will pity me.

*

LA MORT AU PAIEN
Viens, malheureux paien, incrédule pervers!
Insensé, sous des noms divers
tu n'as adoré que le diable,
et lui suel a recu la prière exécrable.

RÉPONSE DU PAIEN
Jupiter, Mars, Neptune, et toi, dieu sombre et triste,
Pluton! Si par bonheur vous etes immortels,
accourez, défendez l'ami de vos autels!
Si vous ne l'etes pas, que Saturne m'assiste.

*

LA MORTE AL PAGANO
Infelice pagano, scettico perverso! Sotto diversi nomi non hai fatto altro che adorare
il diavolo. Ebbene, sembra che abbia ascoltato finalmente le tue preghiere!

RISPOSTA DEL PAGANO
Giove, Marte, Nettuno, e tu, Dio cupo e triste, Plutone! Se davvero siete immortali,
venite a salvare un vostro fedele, altrimenti, che Saturno m'assista.

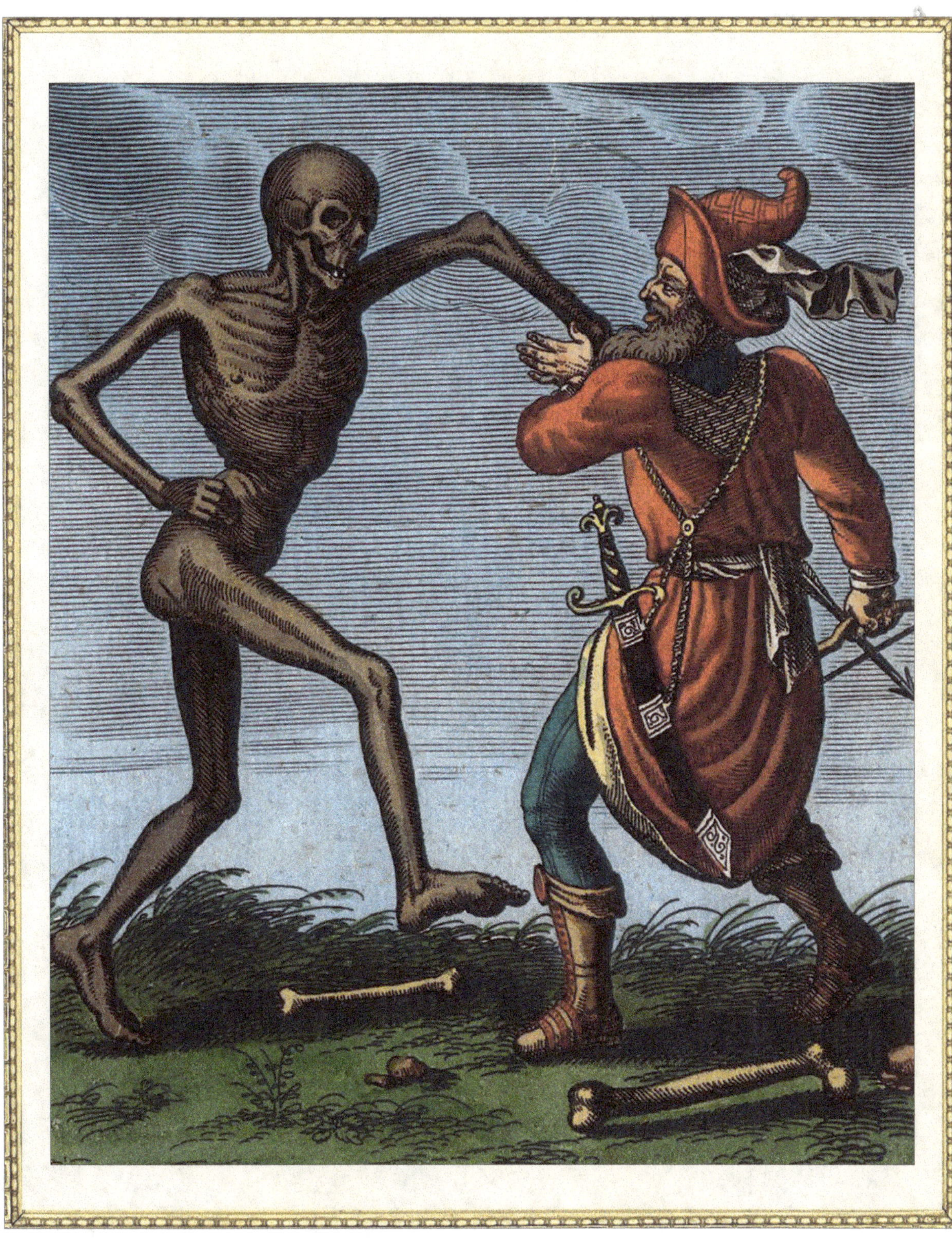

DEATH TO THE PAGANESS

Hark! Paganess I can so gay a dead march on my bag pipe play.
You too must dance to that same strain; you call on all the gods in vain.

THE PAGANESS' REPLY

O Juno, Venus, Pallas, oh! Ye Goddesses some pity shew.
Must I then die? O misery! No charm, I find, from Death can free!

*

LA MORT A LA PAIENNE

Ma musette, je crois, n'est pas sans harmonie;
d'un joli chant de mort je te puis amuser.
Viens danser sur mes pas, et sans cérémonie,
tous les dieux que tu sers n'en peuvent dispenser.

RÉPONSE DE LA PAIENNE

Junon, Venus, Pallas, divinités nombreuses!
Accourez, montrez-moi dans ces cruels instants
si j'ai bien adressé mes offrandes pieuses,
ou si j'ai perdu mon encens.

*

LA MORTE ALLA PAGANA

Sai, Pagana, posso suonare una bellissima marcia funebre con la mia cornamusa.
Dovresti ballare anche tu, invece di invocare invano i tuoi dei.

RISPOSTA DELLA PAGANA

Oh Giunone, Venere e Pallade! Mostratemi un po' di pietà!
Sto per morire, dunque? Oh, miseria! Niente mi può liberare dalla Morte!

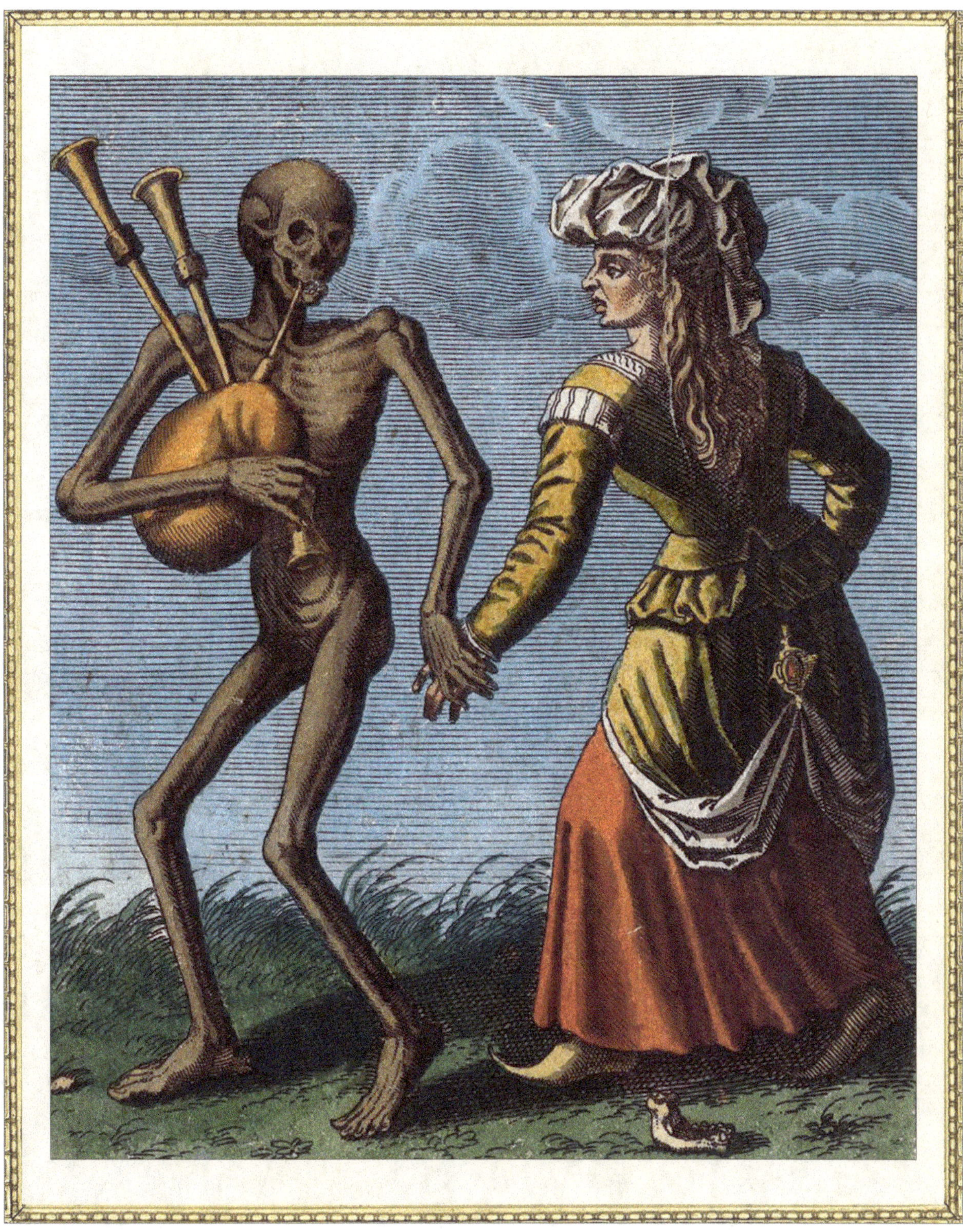

DEATH TO THE COOK

Come here, John Cook, you too must trudge, how fat you've grown, you scare can budge; full many a morsel sweet you've cooked, now all is sour, for you are booked.

THE COOK'S REPLY

Fat capons, geese and fish I've dressed, my master's table oft was pressed. Venison, pastry and sweet cake, to leave you makes my belly ache.

*

LA MORT AU CUISINIER

Viens ca, massive créature,
sur les pas de la mort trainer ton corps épais;
aux lieux où les gourmands font fort sotte figure
tu vas gouter d'un sort moins doux que tes banquets.

RÉPONSE DU CUISINIER

Soigneux de bien nourrir mes hotes et moi meme,
de leur ventre et du mien je m'étais fait un dieu;
mais la mort va bientot m'entrainer dans un lieu
où tous les jours il est careme.

*

LA MORTE AL CUOCO

Forza grassone, immagino sia difficile visto il tuo peso, ma devi arrancare anche tu. Hai preparato molti piatti, ma ora che sono tutti rancidi, sono prenotati per te!

RISPOSTA DEL CUOCO

Grassi capponi, oche e pesci ho preparato e servito alla tavola del mio padrone. Carne di cervo, torte e dolci...al solo pensiero mi viene la nausea!

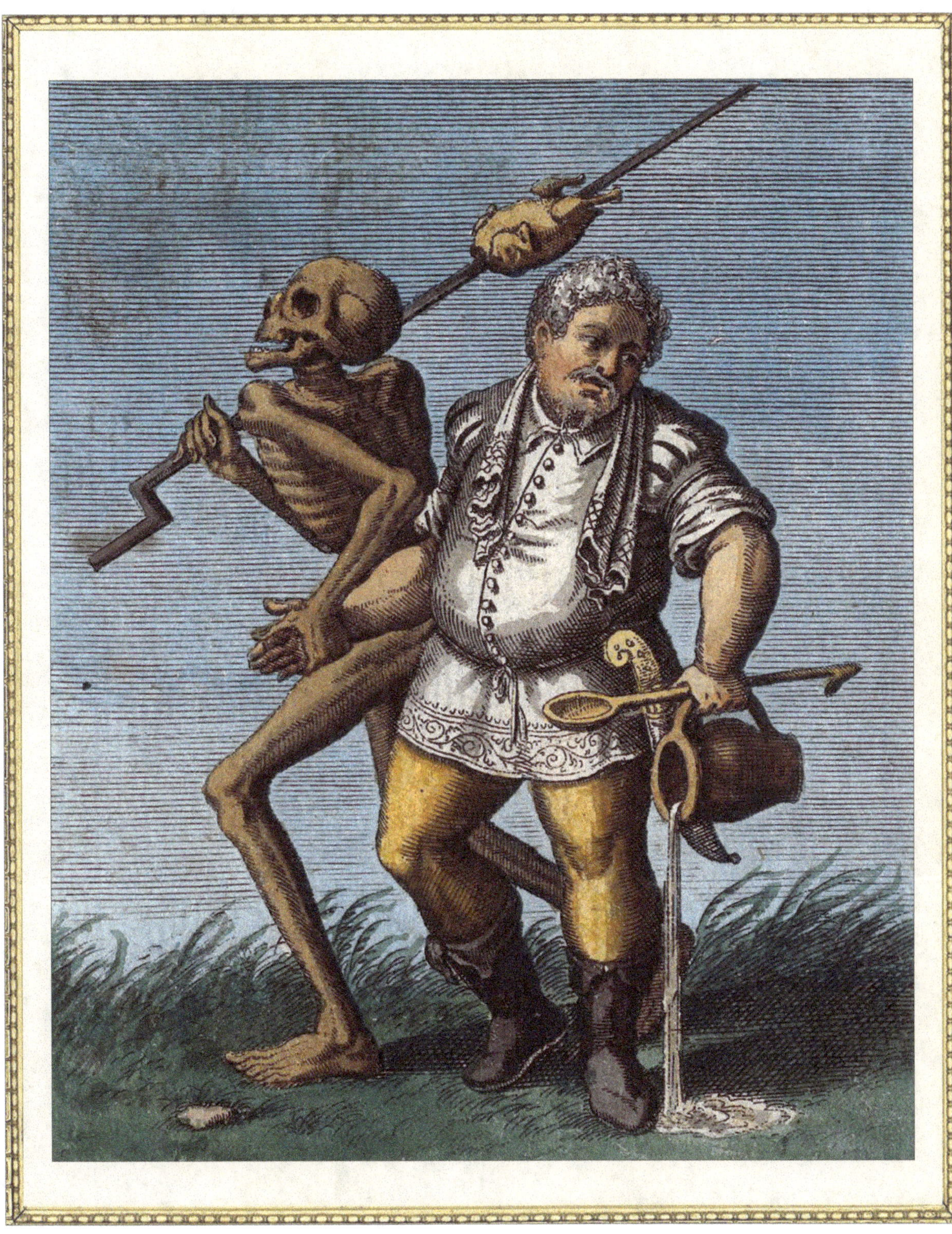

DEATH TO THE PEASANT
You've had your day of toil and sweat and laboured hard from morn till late;
now from your load I'll set you free, basket, flail, sword, give all to me.

THE PEASANT'S REPLY
O Death, give me my hat again, to me my work no more gives pain,
'tis but my task every day; why drag me poor old man away?

*

LA MORT AU PAYSAN
Sous le poids du labeur et d'un dur vasselage
tu ne gémiras plus; je viens t'en décharger;
donne-moi ce fléau, ce sabre, ce bagage:
sans perder un seul instant je veux te soulager.

RÉPONSE DU PAYSAN
Il est vrai, je souffrais; mais, o mort, mort terrible!
Le sort le plus cruel vaut encore mieux que toi;
rends-moi mon bien, mes maux, ma carrière pénible,
eh! Quel cas ferais-tu d'un vilain tel que moi?

*

LA MORTE AL PAESANO
Le tue giornate sono state piene di fatica e sudore, hai lavorato duro dalla mattina
fino a sera. Ti libererò da tutto questo, dalla cesta, la spada, il flagello; dai tutto a me.

RISPOSTA DEL PAESANO
Ti prego, Morte, ridammi il mio cappello! Il mio lavoro non mi provoca dolore, lo
farei ancora ogni giorno. Perché vuoi trascinare via un povero vecchio?

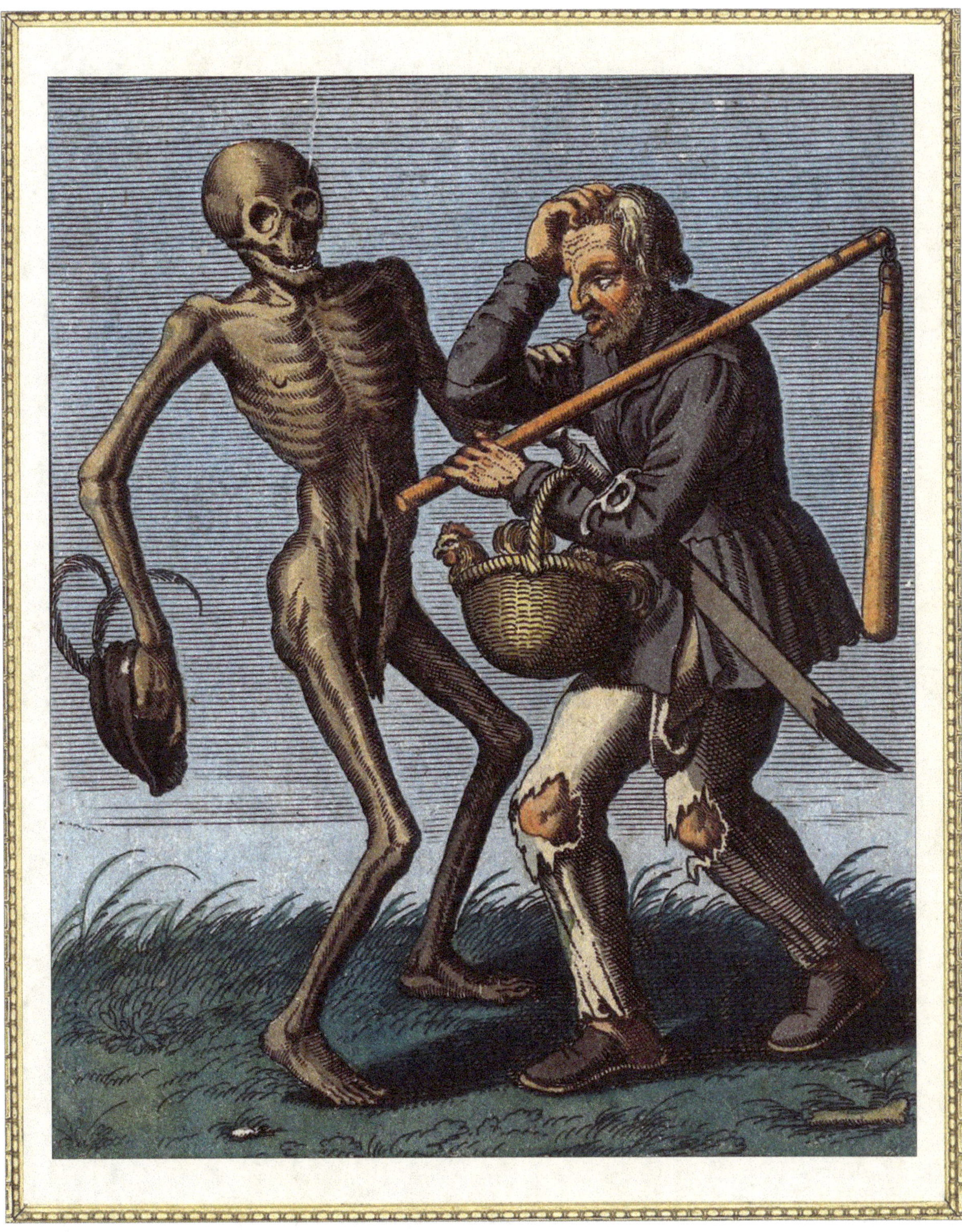

DEATH TO THE PAINTER

Now John Hugh Klauber, cease to paint, on other matters now we're bent;
your skill and labour all are vain when you are called like other men.

THE PAINTER'S REPLY

O God, I pray thee stand by me, since I too from this world must flee;
to thy hand I my sould commend, when comes the hour my life must end.

*

LA MORT AU PEINTRE

Arrete, c'est assez. Ton utile peinture
a retracé le sort de toute créature;
elle a de la mort meme osé saisir les traits.
Ces trais, dans peu de temps, seront ta propre image.

RÉPONSE DU PEINTRE

Puisqu'il faut tout quitter, et mon art et la vie,
assiste-moi, Seigneur, de ta grace infinie,
et daigne recueillir mon ame dans la paix.
Et puissent mes travaux, conserver ma mémoire.

*

LA MORTE AL PITTORE

Smetti di dipingere, è abbastanza. La tua utile pittura ha descritto la sorte di ogni
creatura. Hai dipinto anche un morto, vero? Quello sarà il tuo auto-ritratto ora.

RISPOSTA DEL PITTORE

Se devo lasciare tutto, la mia arte e la mia vita, assistimi, o Signore, e concedimi la
tua grazia. Un ultimo desiderio: possano i miei quadri conservare la mia memoria.

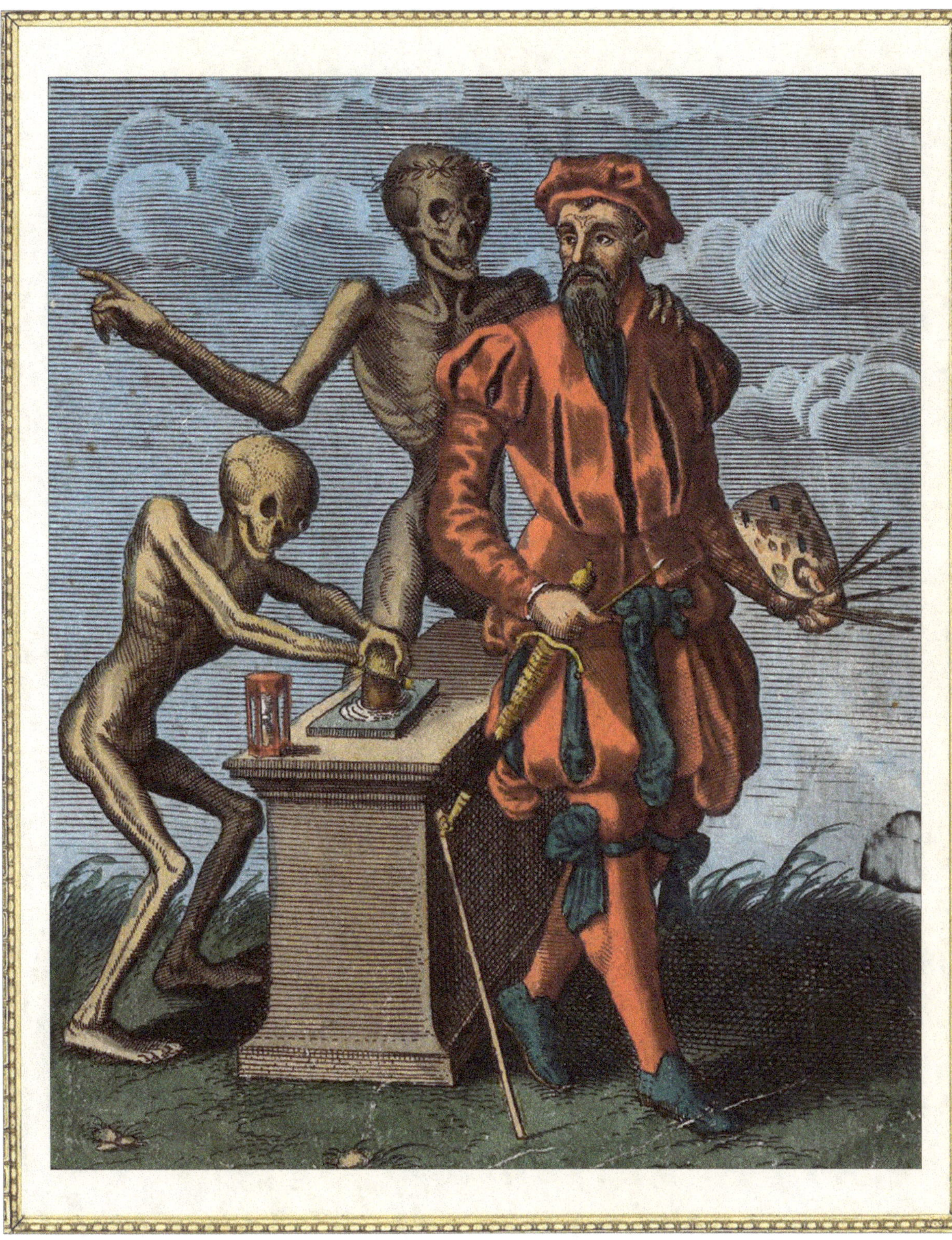

DEATH TO THE PAINTER'S WIFE

Cease now, fond wife, your grief so wild, and follow in my dance your child;
no more you can escape from me, so with your dress-cap I'll make free.

THE PAINTER'S WIFE'S REPLY

O Death, I've long been quite resigned, yet hope eternal life to find,
though his dire grasp me sorely proves and me with man and child removes.

*

LA MORT A LA FEMME DU PEINTRE

Femme au séjour des morts ton enfant te devance;
suis ses pas sans murmure et prends-moi ce berceau
où tu voyais en espérance
s'ébattre sous ta garde un nourrison nouveau.

RÉPONSE DE LA FEMME DU PEINTRE

Époux, épouse, enfant, une familie entière,
sous tes coups redoublés tombent presque à la fois;
mais je n'accuse point ta rigueur salutaire;
tu vas au pied de Dieu nous réunir tous trois.

*

LA MORTE ALLA MOGLIE DEL PITTORE

Donna, il tuo bambino ti fa strada verso la morte. Seguilo senza dire una parola e
lasciami questa culla; la darò ad un nuovo poppante senza speranza.

RISPOSTA DELLA MOGLIE DEL PITTORE

Marito, moglie e bambino: una famiglia intera cade sotto i tuoi colpi nello stesso
momento. Non ti accuso, almeno so che ci ritroveremo ai piedi di Dio, noi tre
riuniti.

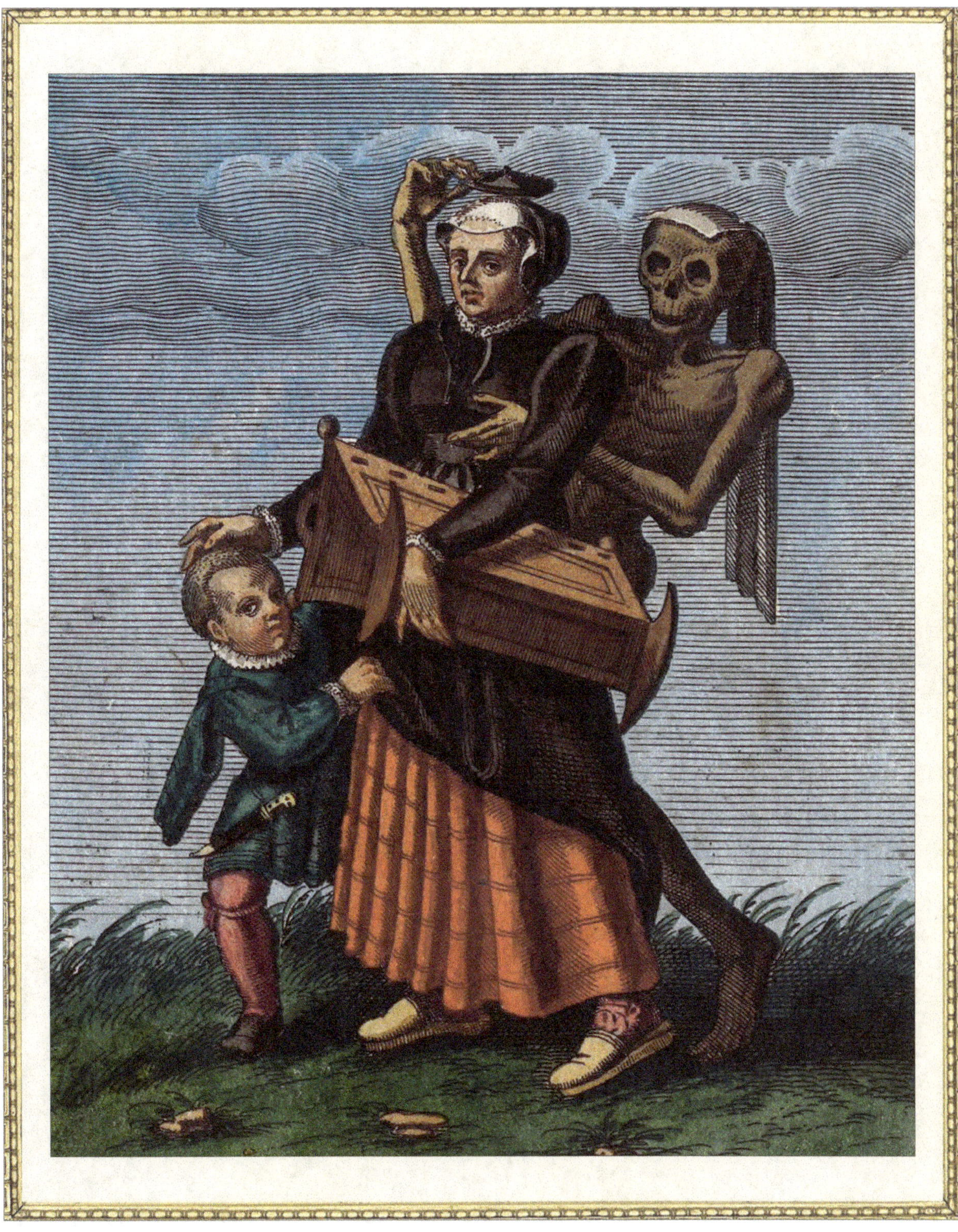

Such the fate of human kind,
life's beginning and life's end,
all of us let duly mind
and to God our souls commend!
Tho' glorious first in Paradise
and full of grace and favour,
yet Adam fell through the fiend's device,
but Christ has come his saviour!

*

Voilà du genre humain l'histoire déplorable,
le démon triomphant, et l'homme criminel;
mais adorez, mortels, le remède ineffable
qu'à des maux sans remède applique l'Éternel.
Réfléchissant sur lui la gloire paternelle,
pur, innocent et beau, vivait ce couple heureux;
mais leur crime, irritant le souverain des cieux,
change en un lieu d'exil cette terre si belle.

*

Ecco la deplorevole storia del genere umano,
il demonio trionfante, e l'uomo criminale;
ma adorate, mortali, il rimedio ineffabile
che ai mali senza rimedio applica l'Eterno.
Riflettendo su lui la gloria paterna,
pura, innocente e bella, viveva questa coppia felice;
ma il loro crimine, irritò il sovrano dei cieli,
il quale rese questa terra solo un luogo d'esilio.

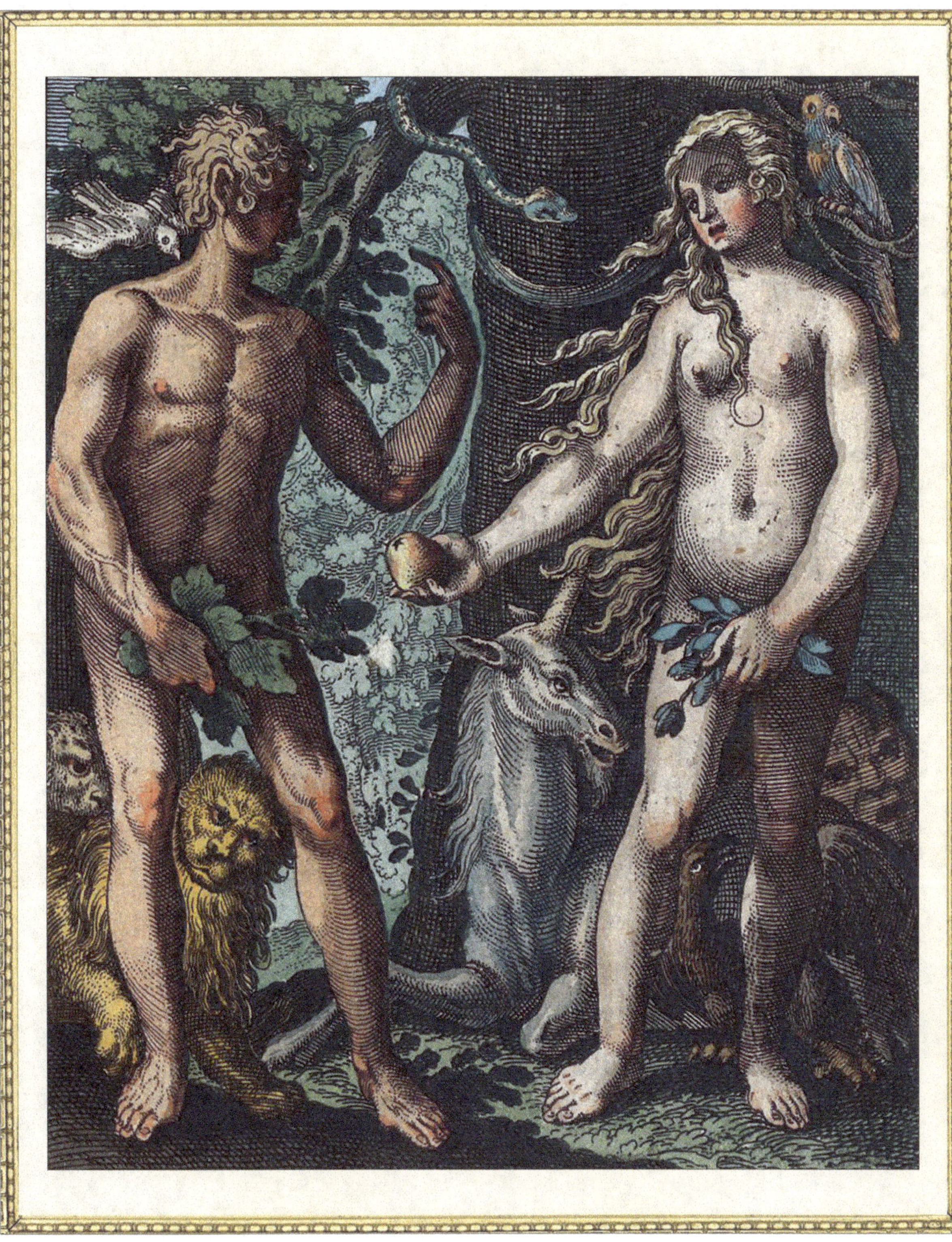

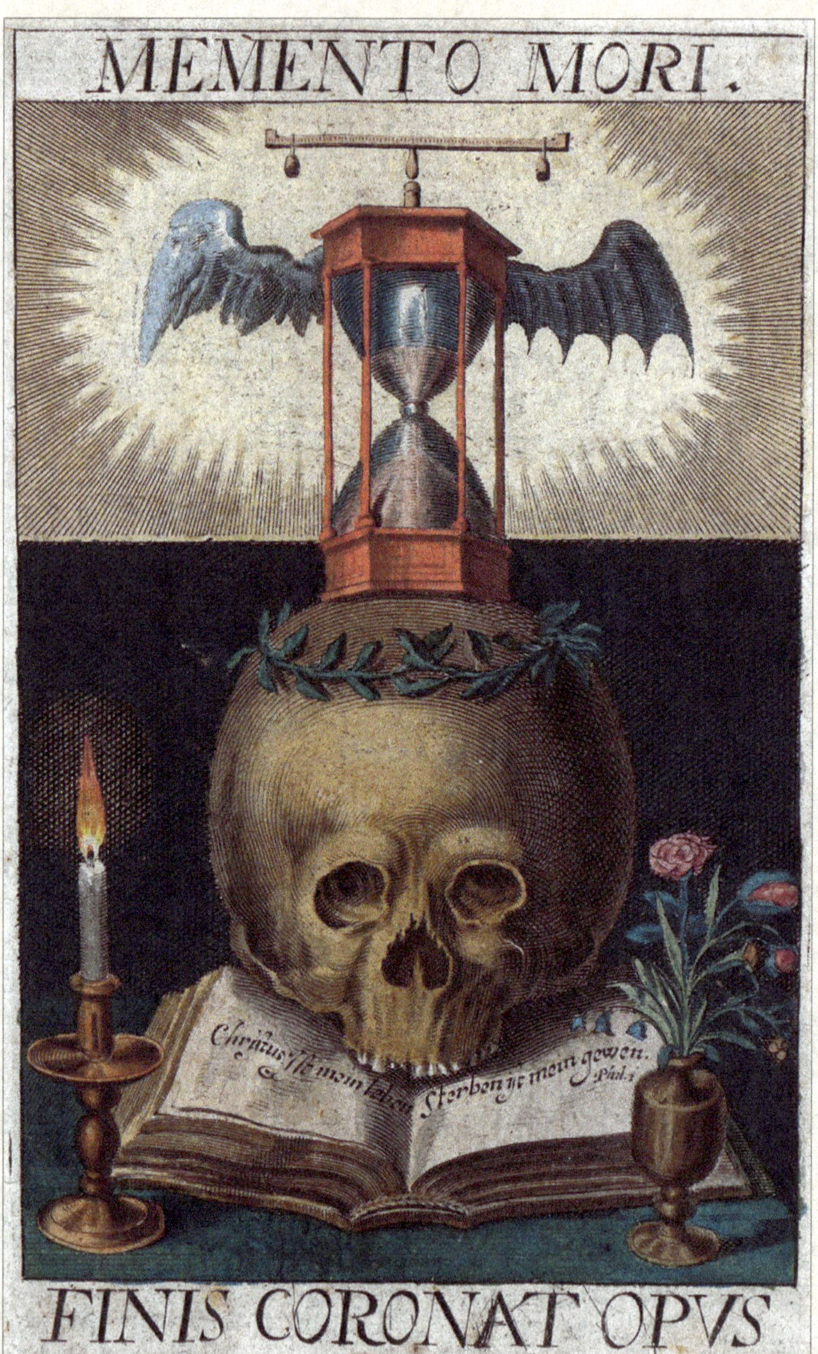

MEMENTO MORI.
FINIS CORONAT OPVS

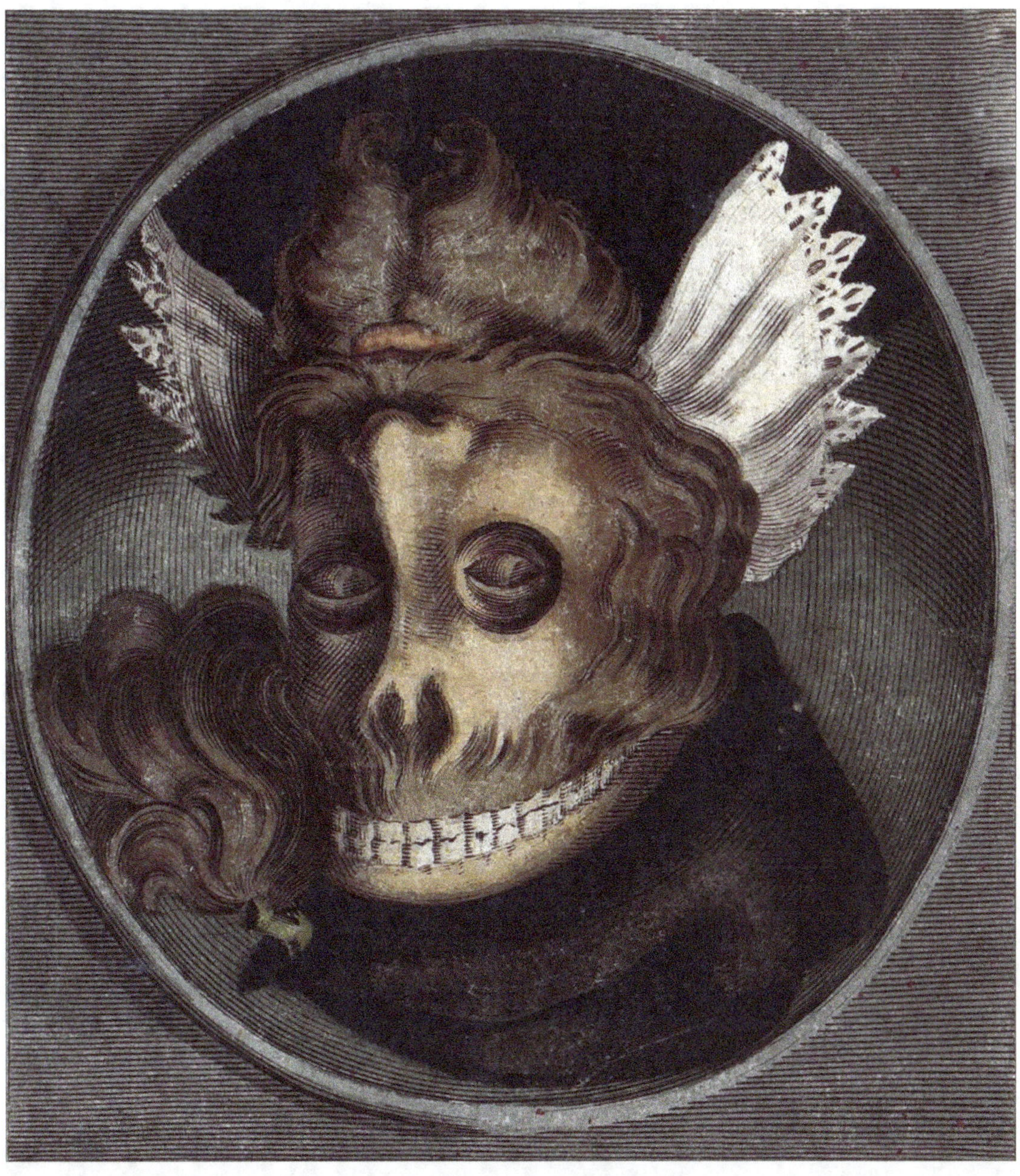

Behold, my fellow man, how wretched, and miserable and pour and blind and naked
I am, and knew it not. Revelation 3

Mais tu ne connais pas que tu es malheureux, misérable, aveugle et nud. Apocal. 3

Ma non sai invece che tu sei infelice, miserabile, cieco e nudo. Apocalisse 3

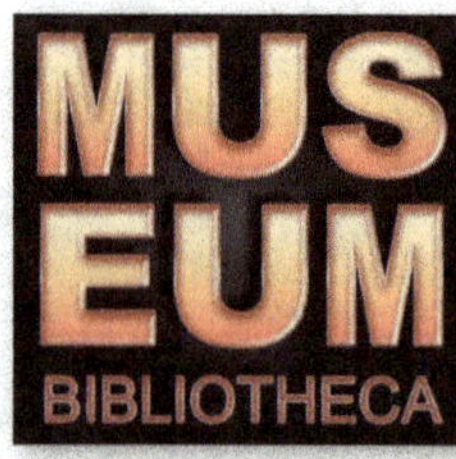